21 Secrets to Eternal Love

Timeless Lessons For Every Generation

Rakesh Dogra

Chennai • Bangalore

CLEVER FOX PUBLISHING
Chennai, India

Published by CLEVER FOX PUBLISHING 2025

ISBN: 978-93-67071-24-3

Contents

Preface

Haven't we all been intrigued by the topic of love for as long as we can remember? Love has inspired poets and authors, created legends, and played an important role in our lives. Yet, love remains one of the most complex and often misunderstood emotions. The very idea of this book, "21 Secrets to Eternal Love: Lessons for Every Generation," is a heartfelt journey exploring the multifaceted nature of love and, in the process, try to shed light on the journey toward meaningful connections and enduring relationships.

Today's world is all about shallow connections, but love can never be seen through a superficial lens. Based on my experience and life journey, let's explore the depths of love that lie beneath the surface of glossy images and instant gratification solutions. In this book, I'm excited to invite you on a heartfelt exploration of love in its many beautiful forms—self-love, family connections, friendships, and the richness of shared experiences. Each chapter would bring insights and reflections designed to resonate with you, no matter where you are on your love journey.

Each of you would have likely experienced love from childhood to the present, carrying a wealth of love in so many forms. Love isn't a one-size-fits-all phenomenon; it flows differently through each person, shaped by our unique individuals, genders, cultures, and more. I feel truly blessed to have received the wonderful love of my parents and siblings. Since then, I've had my share of fleeting romances before finding my amazing life partner, Ritu, who has shown me the true meaning of love. While I'm no love expert, I've made my share of mistakes—just like everyone else—and I'm thankful for the lessons each experience has brought me.

Inspiration for this book has been drawn from my life and the amazing stories of friends, outstanding works from various wonderful writers, classic movies, and timeless wisdom given by great thinkers and writers. Most of the lessons that you will come across here are not just on paper but takeaways drawn from the journeys of countless people who have navigated beautiful paths of love. We will discuss how trust, open communication, vulnerability, and continuous growth cultivate love. I'll share with you heartfelt stories, valuable life lessons, and actionable steps to make your journey of love easier.

As you walk with me through the following pages, I urge you to keep your heart and mind open. Take a moment to reflect on your life and memories, savouring the beauty found in both joy and pain and embrace the important lessons that love teaches us each day. The insights presented here are meant to inspire, guide, and empower you to develop thoughts on love that will raise your spirit and make your relationships in life richer.

Let us not forget that love is not a destination but an amazing journey in which a person can experience moments of endless growth, transformation, and emotional connection. Here's to celebrating the beautiful and extraordinary essence of love! I hope you find secrets within these pages that go straight to the heart, resonate with depth, and get you moving to truly understand relationships at a deeper level.

With warmth and gratitude,

Rakesh Dogra

Acknowledgement

The journey of writing this book has been one of deep introspection, reflection on my experiences, and drawing inspiration to fulfill my dreams of becoming an author. I would like to express my heartfelt gratitude to the Almighty and everyone who helped me turn this dream into reality.

First and foremost, I want to thank my family for their unwavering love, support, and encouragement throughout this process. To my parents, thank you for showing me the true essence of love. To my amazing wife, Ritu, your unconditional love and steadfast belief in me have been my anchor through thick and thin. My lovely children, Nishthaa and Siddharth, your pure love and innocence have provided me with endless energy.

I am profoundly grateful to my friends and colleagues who have consistently supported me and motivated me to explore my creative pursuits. I would also like to give special thanks to my teachers and mentors who selflessly imparted the knowledge that has shaped my present self.

A big thank you to "Inspiring Jatin" for helping me believe in myself and for being a catalyst in turning my dreams into reality.

Finally, I extend my gratitude to my readers for choosing this book to explore the beautiful ways love enters our lives. I'm sanguine that the thoughts I express within these pages will inspire you and resonate with your hearts.

With profound gratitude,

Rakesh Dogra

Introduction

"Secrets to Rediscovering Love: A Journey of Growth, Resilience, and Connection"

In a world where love is often seen as a whirlwind romance, with fleeting moments and fairytale endings, the reality is often much more intricate. Love, in all its forms, is not just about finding "the one"; it is about profound self-understanding and deep connections with others. It is a journey, a cycle, a commitment—an adventure that should be explored.

Let's picture this: Sudha sits on a park bench. Autumn leaves dance around her as if they were the whirlpool of her thoughts, swirling around her. Just days ago, she had ended a relationship that made her heart soar. Today, her mind echoed the emptiness that lingered within her. She saw couples walking by, their fingers intertwined, laughter breaking out like the vivid colours of the season. Their love seemed flawless, immune to doubt or sorrow.

Yet, in that moment of despair, something extraordinary happened. An elderly couple crossed her vision. They walked slowly but with great confidence, their hands clasped together, their smiles lighting up their wrinkled faces. Sudha could overhear bits and pieces of their conversation as they approached- a gentle banter filled with warmth, teasing, and reverence.

"I told you, dear, it's your turn to choose the next movie," the husband chuckled, his eyes sparkling with affection. His wife playfully nudged him, "Only if you promise not to fall asleep this time!" Sudha couldn't help but smile, recognising that their love wasn't perfect; it was genuine. It had withstood numerous storms, embraced imperfections, and thrived through a trail of shared memories.

And just like that, a glimmer of hope ignited in Sudha's heart. Love was not merely the stuff of fairy tales; it encompassed growth, resilience, and the journey of two imperfect souls uniting. As Maya Angelou has beautifully stated, **"Love recognises no barriers. It jumps hurdles, leaps fences, penetrates walls to arrive at its destination full of hope."**

Mythology is replete with Love stories that inspire us through their sagas of devotion and commitment to overcome all odds. Let's explore the enchanting divine love story of Shiva and Parvati, a beautiful tale filled with devotion, perseverance, and a divine bond.

Parvati was a lovely daughter of the mountain king Himavan and his queen Mena. She harboured a deep desire for Lord Shiva, the sage of profound wisdom. From her earliest years, she was enthralled by stories of Shiva's miraculous strength, his immense insight, and his mild nature, all of which drove her to win his heart.

After several years of meditation, Parvati, with a heart full of courage, decided to search for her beloved, who had withdrawn himself into the profound contemplation of the loss of his precious wife, Sati. She took the form of an ordinary mountain maiden to search for Shiva, who lived in the great Himalayas. She went in search of him with fixed devotion and stern penance to show the depth of her love. Each problem she faced only made her more determined, showing how much she actually felt.

Seeing such a resolution, even the gods were moved. They sent Kama, the god of love, to break Shiva's meditation and revive his interest in the world. But Shiva, in his divine wrath, opened his third eye and reduced Kama to ashes. Parvati, though heartbroken, did not waver. She continued her ascetic practices, embodying patience and resilience.

Deeply moved by Parvati's indomitable spirit, Shiva finally emerged from his meditations. He acknowledged her love and revealed himself in a form that would only exist for her; it had been her profound love alone that had kindled Shiva's awakening. A wonderful union was now ecstatically celebrated as a cosmic event, embodying, as it did, a harmony of passion and detachment.

The marriage of Shiva and Parvati is more than a mythological narrative; it is the harmonious union of divine masculine and feminine energies, encouraging devotees to find a balance within their own souls. Their love story endures as a poignant reminder of the strength found in love and devotion, illustrating the extraordinary lengths one will travel for genuine connection, resonating through the ages as an everlasting testament to love's ability to rise above all barriers.

Let's delve into another beautiful story of Satyavan and Savitri, where even God had to relent and bless them in their pursuit of love.

King Ashvapati of Madra, who had always desired children, spent eighteen years doing rigorous penance and true worship of the goddess Savitri. In gratitude to his undeterred worship, she granted him a boon: a daughter would be the origin of a hundred sons. His queen delivered a beautiful daughter whom he named Savitri.

Savitri blossomed into a virtuous woman, loved not only for her beauty but also for her benevolent soul. She chose Satyavan, the deposed prince of Shalva, who lived in a forest with his blind father, King Dyumatsena. Sage Narada had already warned Savitri and Ashvapati that Satyavan would die within a year. However, love did not let Savitri stop her from marrying Satyavan, and she took her new life with great enthusiasm as a devoted hermit in the peaceful forest.

As the fateful day of Satyavan's death was at hand, Savitri fasted and prayed with great intensity for three whole days. On that destined day, she accompanied him into the forest, where he fell into unconsciousness there. It was then that the god of death, Yama, appeared to claim his soul.

Undeterred, Savitri followed Yama with unwavering courage, engaging him in a profound discussion about dharma and virtue. She implored him for Satyavan's life, and, moved by her remarkable strength of character, Yama granted her three wishes, though Satyavan's life was not among them. First, Savitri requested her father-in-law's eyesight; next, she asked for his kingdom; and lastly, she wished to be blessed with a hundred sons alongside Satyavan. Yama consented to her requests, yet he failed to notice one essential detail.

Seizing the moment, Savitri implored that Satyavan's life be restored, thus allowing her final boon to be realised. Moved by her steadfast devotion, Yama graciously granted this request, bestowing upon them the blessing of long and joyful lives together.

Satyavan was restored to life and returned to Savitri. This extraordinary saga of love and resilience has been celebrated over the ages, ***a saga that speaks of Savitri's wisdom and deep commitment that saved her husband and restored harmony to her family.***

In the pages that follow, secret truths of eternal love shall be revealed. Each chapter is saturated with lessons—timeless truths and practical insights—that have the power to change your view of love, whether you are cultivating a lifelong partnership, mending the scars of heartbreak, or embarking on the journey of self-love.

We will take a journey into the very core of love, digging up deep, rich roots of self-acceptance and the significant importance of family ties. Together, we will unravel the complexities of communication, emotional bonds, and strength in vulnerability. As you walk this path, you'll come to understand that love goes beyond just a feeling-it is a dynamic story with threads of shared experience, personal growth, and steadfast support.

This book will explore the creation of relationships that help us and others rise—inspirational relationships that encourage, support, and last a lifetime. Through the strength of connection and selflessness, let us strive to become the type of people who make the world a better place by just being there.

So, let us embark on this journey together. Open your heart, and let's unlock the secrets to eternal love—one lesson at a time. Rediscover the beauty of love, not only in its joy but also in its challenges. By the end, you'll not only understand love better, but you'll also appreciate it more deeply. So, here's to love in all its splendid forms.

PART 1

THE CYCLE OF LOVE

This chapter will explore the basic secrets of eternal love, which are the very core of what feeds our relationships and helps create a beautiful cycle of affection that runs across generations. Love is so intricately woven from the threads of family bonds, self-acceptance, and commitment to personal growth. Together, let's explore the three secrets underlying this cycle.

SECRET 1

"FROM ROOTS TO WINGS: NURTURING FAMILY LOVE THROUGH GENERATIONS"

"Families are like branches on a tree; we grow in different directions, yet our roots remain as one."

– Unknown

Unconditional love of parents

It is this love from our families that beautifully weaves together the threads of our identity. The first moments of a child's existence are wrapped in the gentle warmth of a mother's love. This unique bond, rich with nurturing and affection, establishes the foundation for the child's emotional growth. The presence of a loving mother offers not only physical nourishment but also instils a comforting sense of security, essential for the child's growth. It is in these early years that the essence of love is absorbed, creating the solid foundation upon which the child's personality will be constructed.

The love and affection we have experienced in childhood are the most important foundations that mould our identities into adults and lead us through difficult times. The warmth of that early love prepares us to handle difficulties, stress and anxiety with much ease. A child loved by the unwavering embrace of unconditional love can blossom into a resilient, self-assured individual, fully prepared to face the world around him with unwavering courage.

Just as a mother's love embraces and nurtures, so too does a father's protection play an important role in the development of a child. A father's counselling and strong support foster self-confidence and instil within them a deep sense of self-worth. They learn that they can go through life boldly, facing its challenges, thus equipping themselves to face life with much more courage and resilience.

I can proudly say that my understanding of perceiving and expressing love came from my parents. I have seen love in its purest form through them. So, when I think of how my life partner should love me, I often compare that with my experience. Many think that girls often look for qualities in their partners that are similar to those of their fathers. Similarly, some boys may look for qualities similar to those found in their family relationships.

The impact of family dynamics.

However, the dynamics within a family can profoundly change this story. A child who grows up in a house that is marred by domestic violence or relentless strife comes to view love from a distorted perspective. This pervasive negativity leaves deep imprints on the child's psyche, shaping their comprehension of relationships and presenting obstacles in their emotional bonds as they mature. The atmosphere of the household serves as an unseen force, steering them toward either nurturing relationships or casting lingering shadows that may endure for years.

As children grow, they imbibe values that serve as the pillars of their expressions of love. Empathy, emotional connection, and open communication form the bedrock of healthy relationships, which are inculcated in them through the interaction and behaviour of their parents. These are not lessons in the abstract but are lived experiences that profoundly shape their outlook on love and connection.

Transmission of Love to Future Generations

The exquisite cycle of love continues when these children grow and start their own families. In relationships full of mutual respect and affection, they gently pass on the love that has been bestowed on them. Their homes become havens that welcome in and nurture the planting of positivity, growing the next generation. The legacy of love continues to thrive with ageing parents.

It is but natural for our elderly parents' emotional needs to change with the times, and thus necessitates a little more nurturing and care from us, their grown children. Simple acts of kindness become truly meaningful when they involve being listened to and loved back, which are ways of reinforcing our family ties. **This is indeed a love cycle - truly phenomenal because it spans beyond one generation's action of giving and appreciating the return of love as we pay respect to our ageing parents.**

As a father, I cherish every moment spent with my children, and I strive to share the wonderful gifts of love, care, and guidance that shaped my own childhood. Likewise, I admire Ritu for being such a devoted mother; she truly pours her heart into nurturing our kids and instilling the strong values she learned from her own parents.

Everlasting Connection

Love is such a beautiful, long-lasting bond, like a thread that weaves its way through generations. It moulds us, makes us, and finally defines our capacity to love other people with depth. In embracing love and sharing it, we fulfil the most intrinsic human need, creating waves throughout time as we connect the past, present, and future. Through love, we discover the core of who we are and who we want to be, and we build a world infused with kindness and compassion.

On a warm summer evening, with sunlight filtering through the leaves of her backyard. A young girl named Divya sits on a swing, her mother gently pushing her as their laughter fills the air like a sweet melody. "You can do anything, Divya!" her mother exclaims, her voice ringing with affirmations that resonate profoundly within the girl's heart. Her mother is the epitome of love, instilling treasured values that will remain with her for the rest of her life.

This support blossoms into a deep affection that nourishes Divya's spirit, giving her the confidence to step out into the world.

As Divya grows up, the affection she receives from her family forms the warm foundation upon which she builds her life. She learns that love is something to be cherished and nurtured; it is a beautiful responsibility and something we share as a treasured gift. Years later, she finds herself at the bedside of her ageing parents, tenderly holding their hands and reciprocating all the love they had poured into her life.

In these golden hours, she listens to the tales they tell her, and the gentle cradling of their hands assures them they are valuable and loved in their twilight years. In these simple acts of kindness, Divya learns the truth of love as a beautiful cycle of a joyful exchange that binds one generation to the next.

Ultimately, the lesson comes across beautifully: the love we receive helps shape who we are, and it's our job to pass that love on, ensuring its remarkable continuity and influence.

SECRET 2

EMBRACE YOURSELF: THE FOUNDATION OF SELF-LOVE

"It is only when you have mastered the art of loving yourself that you can truly love others"

– Robin Sharma.

"Your task is not to see for love, but merely to seek and find all the barriers within yourself that you have built against it."

– Rumi.

Understanding Self Love

Self-love is more than just a phrase; it's a powerful practice at the core of our being. It is the unwavering belief in your worth, regardless of others' opinions or the challenges life presents. Have you heard the saying, "You can't pour from an empty cup"? It's a phrase we often acknowledge without fully grasping its deeper meaning. In romantic relationships, self-love is essential. Loving yourself is not a choice; it is the basis of building meaningful and healthy relationships with others.

Self-love is all about valuing yourself, setting boundaries, and embracing your worth, including your little imperfections. It's about becoming your biggest cheerleader and best friend. **When you really embrace self-love, you are telling yourself, "I deserve love, happiness, and all the amazing experiences life has to offer."**

Self-Acceptance

Whether it is playful banter or trying circumstances, always keep in mind not to belittle yourself or undermine your worth. Instead, focus on making gradual improvements every day. Self-acceptance is the key to growing confidence.

You are a glowing source of love and happiness! Instead of expecting others to shower you with love, realise that you have an infinite capacity to give love. You can share it freely with anyone around in your orbit- your family, friends, those in need, or even the stray animals that cross your way. There are numerous souls out there who can be touched by a piece of kindness and warmth. There's nothing quite like the delight that comes from giving. It's an emotion beyond effort which is beautifully weaved together with generous intent and connection. The universe, in all its vastness, is watching over you at all times. Love given to the world comes back to you in so many surprising and joyous ways. You are a unique creation, and when you take time to find and nurture the beauty within you, you tap into a deep well of strength and resilience.

Self-love, indeed, is a journey of profound depth, like a meditative practice that beckons constant growth in one's personal self.

To face the challenges of life, one needs great courage, and in this process of nurturing this love within, you simultaneously become more capable of giving solace to others, even at your most vulnerable moments. **It may sound strange, but instead of thinking of yourself as just a victim, you can be that source of love and encouragement to all around you.**

The Power of Self-Talk

Your inner dialogue is what shapes your self-perception and the way you look at the world around you. The conversations you hold with yourself shape your reality, formulating your beliefs and influencing your perceptions. Embrace a story of hope, one that speaks about abundance in your life and gives you the power to rise above negativity. Whenever your self-talk lifts up your spirit, it leads to profound transformation.

It is amazing how your self-talk can propel you toward positive action and pull you out of a negative spiral. It could be a fitness resolution, a new hobby, leaving a bad habit, gathering the courage to talk to someone special, or anything that your weak inner voice has been denying you.

True growth blossoms when you face and overcome your inner battles. It is a process that brings together the person you are now with the fantastic person you could be. This requires much more than bravery and determination but also the willingness to start that inner journey. It is all about reconstructing and rediscovering your real self in a world that tries to define you otherwise.

Love the Person in the Mirror

In the end, this journey illuminates the beautiful purpose of life: to love and support the person reflected back at you. Love yourself as a fundamental value, and you will see it blossom in every part of your existence. As you tend to yourself with kindness, the positive energy you create spreads outward, reshaping your reality and touching the lives of others.

Love yourself totally because you deserve all the beauty in this world.

As you start this great journey, remember that the love you nurture within yourself will spill out and make your life richer and those of many more. How others treat or perceive you is built from how you love yourself. Consider this: If you wouldn't respect your own boundaries or value your own worth, then on earth can you expect someone else to do it for you?

Let us take a moment and reflect on Anushka's journey. For many years, she tried to get validation from the world around her, trying desperately to fit into standards that did not ever really capture the essence of who she was. Every smile she had feigned and every compliment she had pursued left her with a heavy, empty heart. Often, she was criticised for her weight, and this filled her with feelings of rejection and exhaustion.

Then, everything shifted for Anushka when she encountered Neerja at a college festival.

Neerja radiated confidence and empowerment, elegantly confronting her own struggles with weight. She enlightened Anushka to the profound truth that her worth was not governed by the opinions of others. This epiphany was as invigorating as sunlight piercing through a turbulent sky. Anushka discovered that self-love is the deepest expression of validation.

It is the reassuring inner voice that reminds us we genuinely deserve respect and joy. This beautiful journey reveals that self-love is not a destination, but rather a nurturing practice that develops over time. While tending to our well-being, we automatically draw in authentic connections and relationships that mirror the love we hold within.

PRACTISING SELF LOVE

- ***Practice self compassion.***
- ***Establish daily affirmation routine.***
- ***Self care.***
- ***Set boundaries.***
- ***Surround youseelf with positivity.***
- ***Celebrate your achievements.***
- ***Practice mindfulness.***
- ***Embrace imperfectios and uniqueness.***
- ***No negative self talk.***
- ***Create gratitude list.***

SECRET 3

MAGNETISING LOVE: VALUES, GROWTH, AND MANIFESTING CONNECTION

"Whatever we plant in our subconscious mind and nourish with repetition and emotion will one day become a reality."

– Earl Nightingale.

"Love isn't finding someone to live with. It's finding someone you can't live without."

– Unknown

Attracting Love: The Next Step in Your Journey

Once you accept the love of self and commit to the path of growth, you'll find yourself capable of giving love as well as worthy of receiving it. The next crucial step in this journey is to attract the love you want into your life. That brings us to a great concept: attracting love.

As we move through the process of adolescence into young adulthood, our minds often wander to dreams of love and what we hope to find in our partners. Such hopes are filled with bright images and heartfelt desires. For many of us, the ideal life mate comes with a number of desired qualities.

The Dream: What We Desire in a Mate

Girls often have a special wish list for their ideal partners! *In my conversations with my wife, she tells me she had a special list of qualities she looked for in her dream man, and many of her friends had the same. (I'm glad she feels that I did tick most of the boxes.)* Women may envision a man who represents:

- Charming and handsome - Affectionate and loving - Respectful and intelligent
- Trustworthy and committed - Supportive of their dreams and ambitions, cheering them on
- Strong, both physically and mentally - Witty, sharing laughs together
- Open and vulnerable for deep emotional connections - Understanding of their quirks and imperfections. A true partner who complements and lifts them up.

Boys have their own unique dreams and desires when it comes to an ideal partner. They might envision that special girl who is:

- Curious and captivating, with a bright intellect; Compassionate, dependable, and truly devoted;
- A wonderful homemaker, overflowing with love, Enjoying life to the fullest, excited to share adventures together - Confident about her own abilities
- A great cook - A like-minded person who clicks with you - Positive Attitude

Manifestation: Calling Your Soulmate to Life

I am sure many of you are familiar with the interesting concept of manifestation. It is basically a deliberate act of bringing your dreams into reality by realigning your thoughts, feelings, and beliefs into the qualities you desire. Attracting your soulmate can indeed be such a fun journey of manifestation! Let us together discover how to elegantly navigate this fascinating process:

1. Define Desired Qualities:

Reflect intently on the qualities you seek in a life partner. Ponder the traits that resonate with your values, aspirations, and ideals. Create a vivid mental picture of these characteristics without becoming fixated on any specific individual.

2. Envision Your Desire:

Imagine yourself already basking in the love of a person having all these attributes. Then, feel the feelings resulting from the perfect relationship - happiness, support, camaraderie, and love. The sharper and the brighter your view, the stronger your manifestation.

3. Release and have patience:

Having a mental image of what you want, now is the time to develop patience. Let manifestation happen at its own pace. Have faith that the Universe knows when the right person will come into your life and will bring that person to you at the right time. Do not rush into relationships or settle for anything less than you really deserve.

4. Be Open and Ready

Wait for love to find you, but in the meantime, be open to opportunities. Do things that you believe in and are worth your while. Get yourself into situations that will bring you the kind of people you can relate with. Prepare yourself to receive love.

5. Never get into dysfunctional relationships.

It is important to stay alert in this journey. Do not give into the pressure of getting into a relationship just because of the fear of loneliness or to speed up the experience. Rushing into love can create unhealthy relationships and devalue your self-image. Instead, take the time to find a relationship that truly enriches your existence.

Conclusion: The Journey of Attracting Love

Embracing love in your life is a beautiful journey that starts with the discovery of who you are and setting clear intentions. As you fine-tune your dreams by focusing on the qualities that resonate with your heart and practising the virtue of patience, you will graciously open yourself to the love that is destined for you. Trust in the universe's timing, and always keep in mind that you deserve a partnership that mirrors your essence and aspirations.

As you welcome love into your life, bear in mind that love transcends the simple act of seeking that perfect partner; it encompasses nurturing a relationship built on mutual respect, support, and shared aspirations. Embrace this journey with an open heart, and you'll discover how effortlessly fulfilling connections flow into your life.

Love has an irresistible pull towards authenticity and personal growth. When we synchronise our values and dreams with our genuine selves, we generate a vibrant energy that beckons love into our lives. The journey of inviting love isn't merely about discovering another; it's about blooming into someone worthy of that deep and meaningful love.

Conclusion of Part 1

Let us pause while reflecting on how the love cycle begins within us and how it radiates in such a beautiful way so that we can embrace our families and generations yet to come. It is all a journey of love received and cultivated within ourselves and all the values that we have in store. With these three simple secrets, we build on a solid foundation to experience enduring love while allowing and nurturing connection, self-acceptance, and growth within our lives. Moving forward together, I pray that these heartfelt principles can light your way to a richer understanding of the extraordinary cycle of love.

PART 2

BUILDING AND NURTURING RELATIONSHIPS

Beautifully woven in the fabric of life are friendships and relationships within the realm of love. Such bonds are beyond just biology or romance; they create the intricate fabric of our human experience. Nurturing, understanding, and mutual respect all work to help relationships thrive. This chapter discusses the essential secrets to cultivating and sustaining lifetime relationships.

SECRET 4

CULTIVATING FRIENDSHIP: BUILDING BONDS THAT LAST

"Love without friendship is like a kite, aloft only when the winds are favourable. Friendship is what gives love its wings."

– Sherry Thomas.

Few colours shine as brightly or endure as magnificently as friendship within the beautiful spectrum of human relationships. While romantic love tends to be the most widely highlighted, the stable foundation of friendship underpins much of our most valued and lasting romantic relationships. Resilient, authentic, and deeply fulfilling love begins with friendship.

Friendship stands out as one of the truest forms of companionship. Friends have that very rare ability to see through our facades. They give an understanding that transcends the mere interaction level, where people constantly feel they have to be on their best behaviour. A real friend accepts you whole and complete, quirks, flaws, and all, including insecurities. They create a haven of vulnerability, making it easy for you to express your innermost thoughts and emotions.

I spent my formative years in a boys' hostel at a boarding school, where I found that friends can truly be our greatest support and strength during tough times. Looking back, I feel proud to say that many of my classmates and friends have really helped shape my personality and stood by me through those challenging moments. Even during my training at the Military Academy, my friends offered the most incredible support.

I've always believed that my life partner would also be my best friend—someone with whom I can share anything and feel her unwavering support in every situation. And she has definitely proven me right! We are each other's best friends and can share everything and anything with one another without hesitation.

Building a Strong Relationship Through Friendship

When two people start their romantic journey with each other, the foundation of friendship profoundly influences the growth of that relationship. A friend being a partner gives an exceptional advantage in a world usually characterised by pretence. There is this extraordinary comfort in knowing you can be completely open and authentic to someone. You don't need to put up any walls; you can be open about who you are and your vulnerabilities.

Romantic love tends to come with lofty expectations, while friendship creates a gentle and easy atmosphere. You can always turn to your friend when things are difficult and find comfort in his or her presence without the tension of being judged. Friendships usually escape the heavy burdens of expectation that can sometimes weigh on relationships. In its most simple sense, companionship is lovely and straightforward: each person supports the other, free from the weight of romantic obligation.

Friendship adds a delightful layer to the complexities of romantic love. Essentially, you're not just lovers; you're each other's biggest supporters! This incredible partnership can make your journey together much more joyful and easier to navigate.

Trust: The Bedrock of Bonding

Trust is one of the cornerstones of any relationship, especially friendship. A friend is likely to depend on you when they need something or you on them in such times. This interdependency brings about a sense of security in the emotional realm as both individuals are held secure and supported.

Conflicts tend to resolve themselves with a sense of warmth and mutual understanding among friends. There flows between them a bond of shared understanding and empathy, which transforms disagreements into opportunities for growth and learning together instead of perceiving them as threats.

Helen Keller beautifully expressed this idea when she said, "**Walking with a friend in the dark is better than walking alone in the light.**" This highlights how essential good friends are in helping us navigate life's uncertainties together.

The Healing Power of Friendship

Life, after all, presents problems, but it's only in these trying moments that the essence of a true friend shines out. True friends walk with you at your darkest moments and help you find a comforting shoulder and a listening ear. These beautiful moments of support will lift your burdens, refresh your spirit, and leave you feeling lighter and full of hope—just as a breath of fresh air on a stormy day.

Having a friend to rely on in times of hardship can change everything. They offer not only emotional support but also priceless perspective. Friends often see things more clearly than we do, and their insights can light our way at difficult times. This kind of support is better than sympathy; it represents a true commitment to our emotional well-being.

Dynamics of Expectations vs. Acceptance

In the realm of romantic relationships, sometimes expectations can become straining pressures. In friendship, however, it works the other way around. While with friends, overt expectation is replaced by pure acceptance. There is no necessity to work for something specific; we just exist together.

You actually really care for each other, and friendships give you a great feeling that you do not have to solve each other's problems. There is a beautiful understanding that both friends can support each other's journeys while growing individually.

This natural dynamic fosters a deeper connection, one that can endure the test of time. As the beautiful saying goes, **"A friend is someone who knows all about you and still loves you."** Such unconditional acceptance fortifies the bond between friends, rendering their relationship all the more resilient.

The Final Thought

Building lasting friendships is not merely a wonderful journey to embark upon; it is, in fact, vital in establishing a robust foundation of love and support in our lives. Friendships really enrich our romantic relationships in terms of safety, comfort, understanding, and even joy. What is absolutely beautiful about these connections is their simplicity: they are straightforward yet profoundly fulfilling.

As Ralph Waldo Emerson wisely stated, **"The only way to have a friend is to be one."** This profound truth echoes profoundly within the realm of relationships—cultivating our friendships is essential for discovering enduring love. Dedicate time to invest in your friendships and observe how they can positively impact various aspects of your life, transforming the journey of love into one rich with shared laughter, resilience, and steadfast support. It will have no bounds when friendship becomes the basis of love because then the growth and happiness are limitless. So let us not miss those friendships that have helped to shape us, those bonds that have stood through time's trials, and the laughter that lights our hearts as we seek to hold on to love forever.

Each relationship built on the basis of friendship creates the potential for the love we will carry with us in life. Friendship makes life rich because love is not just a romantic feeling but something that grows with companionship and shared experiences.

Key Takeaways on Friendship in Relationships

- Friendship as a Foundation: True friendship creates a strong foundation for romantic relationships, offering authenticity, vulnerability, and mutual understanding.
- Safe Space for Vulnerability: Friends provide a judgment-free space where individuals can express their thoughts and emotions openly.
- Trust as the Core: Trust forms the bedrock of friendship, fostering emotional security and support in relationships.
- Reduced Expectations, Increased Acceptance: Friendships are less burdened by societal or romantic expectations, allowing both individuals to feel accepted as they are.
- Conflict Resolution with Empathy: Disagreements in friendships are often approached with understanding and viewed as opportunities for growth.
- Support During Challenges: Friendships shine brightest during difficult times, offering emotional support and a fresh perspective.
- Mutual Growth and Encouragement: A friendship-based relationship supports individual growth while strengthening the collective bond.
- Unconditional Acceptance: In true friendship, acceptance goes beyond flaws, fostering a resilient and enduring connection.

SECRET 5

THE GIFT OF UNCONDITIONAL LOVE: GIVING WITHOUT LIMITS

"Love knows no limits; it is boundless and infinite, expanding our hearts and enriching our lives."

– Rumi.

"True love is actually when your love for that person exceeds your need for that person."

Once you find yourself in love, your entire being becomes devoted to your beloved's happiness, with no thought of receiving anything in return. You can truly love someone only when you embrace them wholly, just as they are. Accept the individual for their true self. Love them without conditions. Become the source of their joy and steadfast support during challenging moments. Be so engrossed in loving them unconditionally that you find no room in your heart to anticipate anything in return.

Essence of Unconditional Love

Unconditional love is such a beautiful, almost magical idea. We find it in poetry, movies, and our lives every day, but truly putting it into practice may reveal its depth and complexity. At its core, however, it is that spirit of eternal love: the resilient kind that would stand against time and hardships, remaining constant even at the worst of times and in moments of imperfection. Let us delve into the true essence of unconditional love. In its simplest form, it entails loving someone wholeheartedly and without reservations. There are no ulterior motives, no anticipation for them to reciprocate your affection, and no criteria that determine whether they are "worthy" of your love.

It is one that perseveres, especially during those moments when perhaps they are feeling a little not so lovable—be it a particularly difficult day or simply not at the best. But this certainly does not mean that one should tolerate toxic behaviour or sacrifice personal well-being. Unconditional love does not equal being a martyr; it is the expression of celebrating the beautiful imperfections of your partner while remaining very firm on healthy boundaries. It is love in the purest form, undiluted by judgment and overflowing with compassion.

The most wonderful thing about unconditional love is its incredible ability to create emotional safety. Imagine being in someone's life who deeply embraces you, flaws and all. They do not hold grudges and keep a mental score of your mistakes. They will never threaten to withdraw their love should you stumble. Instead, they create a sanctuary where you may be yourself, grow, and sometimes stumble along the journey. This level of acceptance creates an environment where both of them can thrive side by side. Now, let's think for a moment about how this speaks to the concept of eternal love. Relationships are intrinsically dynamic; people grow, circumstances change, and obstacles are inevitable.

Conditional Love Vs Unconditional Love.

Conditional love—the kind that depends on certain behaviours, appearances, or achievements—tends to falter when faced with life's uncertainties. But unconditional love adapts. It evolves alongside the people involved because it's rooted in something deeper than surface-level traits or temporary conditions.

Let's think about the honeymoon phase of a relationship. In those early days, everything feels so effortless and magical! You are drawn effortlessly to each other's good qualities and make light of those little imperfections, but that is when, as a relationship deepens, a spark will probably fade a little and make way for the rhythms of life. You may feel that quirks that once made you feel joyful now begin to annoy you. The piling of stress, arguments, and responsibilities brings difficult moments to your relationship. Here, unconditional love really shines its light. It helps guide you through the tough stuff, all while keeping very much the essence of why you chose each other in the first place. Unconditional love has an incredible ability to create a sense of mutual understanding.

If a person feels truly seen and accepted, they are more likely to return that kind and patience in kind. This creates a beautiful cycle that deepens the relationship between partners. Naturally, this doesn't mean that every moment will be flawless. However, it does mean that you'll approach conflicts with empathy instead of defensiveness, focusing on finding a resolution rather than simply striving for victory in an argument.

Boundaries in Unconditional Love

Let's clear up a common misconception: Unconditional love doesn't imply accepting everything without any questions.

It's not a free pass for bad behaviour or a reason to overlook red flags. Healthy relationships thrive through respect, accountability, and hard work. When these three crucial elements are in place, unconditional love becomes the adhesive that elegantly holds everything together. It reminds us gently that we are all imperfect human beings doing the best we can; love isn't about finding perfection but graciously accepting our flaws with warmth.

Cultivating Unconditional Love

Consider the couples you've observed, those who appear to share an unbreakable connection. And there would surely be a few of them around you as well. It's likely that they have perfected the skill of loving one another without conditions. They have come to appreciate each other's idiosyncrasies with laughter rather than criticism. They've discovered the power of swift forgiveness and the importance of open communication. They do not anticipate that their partner will indulge every whim or solve every problem; instead, they nurture each other's growth and enjoy each other's uniqueness. Their love does not depend on the other person's behaviour or lack thereof.

But how does one start practising unconditional love? It is not something that happens overnight. It is a practice, a choice you reaffirm time and again. Here are some ways to get started on this path:

1. **Practice empathy**. Try to see things from your partner's perspective, even if you disagree. Understand that their feelings and lives are valid even though they may be different from yours.
2. **Drop expectations.** You have hopes and dreams for the relationship but do not put rigid expectations on your partner. Allow them the chance to be who they are, not who you think they ought to be.
3. **Cultivate gratitude**. Focus on the things you love and appreciate about your partner, especially during challenging times. Gratitude shifts your Love.
4. **Forgive freely**. Holding onto grudges only creates distance. Practice forgiveness, not because the other person is always "right," but because love is more important than being right.
5. **Love from the inside out.** The more I invest in self-love and acceptance, the easier it is to do for those around me.

6. **Communicate** openly, honestly, and vulnerably about your thoughts, emotions, and needs. And that's where unconditional love grows best, in spaces of trust and understanding.

Final Thoughts

Ultimately, it is essential to remember that unconditional love transcends grand gestures and big declarations. It glimmers brilliantly in those small, everyday instances: the patience you exhibit during difficult conversations, the gentle warmth conveyed through your touch, and your kind willingness to listen without passing judgment. It resides in the way you express "I love you"—not merely with words, but through your thoughtful actions, and in your decision to remain steadfast even when challenges present themselves.

In fact, unconditional love is the only way to forever love because it goes beyond what is fleeting and shallow. It's not about holding on to the past or getting all anxious for the future but just being fully present in that moment and loving totally in the moment. Such love grows deeper with time as it weathers the storms and celebrates the good moments together. It's that kind of love that doesn't just survive but prospers, and then a connection is woven together that feels both timeless and unbreakable.

So, if you're on a journey to uncover the secret to lasting love, begin right here: Love without conditions. Love wholeheartedly—even when it feels a touch vulnerable. Love in a way that uplifts heals and inspires. By embracing this, you'll not only discover the beauty of enduring love but also experience the magnificent transformative power of unconditional love itself.

SECRET 6

EMOTIONAL DEEP-DIVING: CRAFTING LASTING CONNECTIONS

"The best and most beautiful things in this world cannot be seen or even heard but must be felt with the heart."

– Helen Keller

In a world of transient interactions and shallow relationships, the quest for lifelong love can feel like such an arduous endeavour. But one of the beautiful mysteries of making a connection stand the test of time lies in what we call emotional deep-diving. That is going way beyond surface moments of vulnerability or earnest exchanges.

It is a warm journey of discovering each other's emotional terrains- an enriching commitment to genuinely and profoundly understand the depths of feelings, fears, dreams, and vulnerabilities. When such an approach is tender and delicate, it forms that bond that feels so intense that it seems unbreakable.

Love frequently commences at a superficial level. Those first dates, the shared laughter, and that initial spark of attraction resemble the glimmering waves of an ocean—captivating yet ephemeral. Just as waves are influenced by shifting winds, surface-level connections can be swayed by external circumstances. True love, however, beckons us to go deeper—exploring beyond the obvious and into the serene, enduring depths that lie beneath. It is here that the enchantment of emotional deep-diving truly unfolds.

The Underpinnings of Emotional Deep-Diving

Emotional deep-diving is embracing vulnerability and trust. Love grows in a place of trust, and that grows when we are safe enough to let down our guard and be ourselves. Yet, we know that's quite a task! It takes a genuine effort from both parties to feel the feeling of safety. Instead of judgment; we can create curiosity; instead of criticism, we can understand; instead of dismissing each other, we can open our hearts to engagement.

Consider this: how frequently do you inquire of your partner, "How are you?" only to settle for a brief "I'm fine" in reply? Emotional deep-diving transforms those mundane moments into exquisite chances for connection. It tells you to listen—truly listen to the words that frequently remain unspoken. It involves noticing the subtle signals, such as a pause in their voice or a slight sag in their shoulders, and gently prompting them to reveal more.

This process requires patience. People don't reveal their inner selves overnight. Some carry wounds of their past experiences and fear of being judged that makes trust difficult; others may not even realise what lies beneath their surface. However, if you consistently show up with empathy and a willingness to explore, it sends a clear message: you're in it for the long haul. The sunshine, yes, but also the storms.

Unravelling Emotional layers

Emotionally exploring is a gentle process of peeling back layers of your partner's world. All of us don masks - be it in the workplace, among friends, or even within the confines of our homes. True love beckons to gently reveal those layers. It is not just knowing what your partner does but understanding the 'why' that lies behind it. What makes them passionate? What fears and dreams lie within them, perhaps unspoken?

So next time you want to get closer to that someone special of yours, ask subtle questions.

" What makes you truly feel recharged, joyous and relaxed?

"Places to go travelling in bucket list?

"What are your deep-rooted fears you would want to let go of?"

"Who have been your biggest influences in life?"

"What childhood memory makes you smile?"

"What is a dream you have longed to chase yet hesitated to embrace?"

These are not just conversation starters; they beckon a deeper understanding. The responses reveal the emotions and convictions that shape your partner's identity. Listening means embracing their stories without passing judgment or feeling the need to solve their problems. It's about observing their journey and, in that very act, strengthening your connection.

What women want

Although it may seem like a difficult question for all the gentlemen out there, these answers are rarely simple and straightforward. Still, I would like to stick my neck out and say that for many women, forming an emotional connection is the ultimate goal in a relationship with a partner. In addition, **feeling safe with the man she loves is incredibly important to her**. She wants to see a relationship where he keeps her safe from outside dangers, making sure her welfare comes above everything while seeking to create a stress-free zone where abuse and harm might not even be a thought.

Commitment is equally essential; she will cherish the promise that he will not betray her confidence or make her feel insecure by lavishing attention on other women. When a woman has confidence in these three, she can truly open herself to him, free of the fear of being hurt.

The Power of Vulnerability

Many people frequently believe that love revolves around strength, yet the reality is that it is our vulnerability that genuinely fosters connection. To dive deep emotionally means permitting your partner to witness your cracks, scars, and struggles. **It involves declaring, "This is me with my flaws," while trusting that they will accept you just as you are—perhaps even love you more for it.**

Vulnerability is not merely a fleeting occurrence; it is a habit we nurture over time. It involves acknowledging your fears rather than masking them with a facade of bravery. It means revealing those seemingly trivial thoughts you might otherwise dismiss as "silly." It's permitting yourself to weep, even if you've been conditioned to believe that tears represent frailty.

Who says men don't cry? Men also feel vulnerable and tend to forge moments of sincere honesty, thereby creating a foundation for true intimacy.

Naturally, embracing vulnerability entails its own set of risks. What if they judge you? What if they choose to distance themselves? This is precisely why emotional deep-diving truly thrives when both partners are devoted to one another. It becomes a shared journey. When both of you arrive with honesty and compassion, the fear of rejection begins to fade away. Together, you forge a safe harbour where each of you can be seen and loved exactly as you are.

The Impact of Emotional Deep-Diving

As such, when both partners embark on this extraordinary journey of delving deep into their own emotions, the advantages run well beyond the confines of their relationship. You can sleep peacefully with no doubts about one another's intent. Misunderstandings will turn into splendid opportunities for growth rather than becoming just sources of argument. Most importantly, your relationship becomes a cosy sanctuary- a haven where you both feel profoundly valued, cherished, and understood. This robust bond alters the way you confront life's challenges. Life has a way of throwing curveballs, and even the strongest relationships may encounter their share of storms. Yet, with a firm foundation of emotional connection, those storms become significantly easier to navigate. You already know how to communicate, support each other, and navigate your way back after a tough time disagreement.

Ready to give emotional deep-diving a try? Here are some practical steps:

- **Make Time**: Carve out regular, distraction-free moments to connect.
- **Ask Better Questions**: Move beyond "How was your day?" and ask things like, "What's been on your mind lately?"
- **Listen Actively**: When your partner speaks, don't just understand. Reflect back on what you hear so they feel seen.
- **Lead with Vulnerability**: Share something personal. It sets the tone and invites your partner to do the same.

- **Be Patient**: Trust takes time. If your partner is hesitant, don't push. Show them through actions that they can trust you.
- **Celebrate Wins**: Acknowledge moments of connection. Gratitude reinforces the behaviour.

Why It Matters

Eternal love has nothing at all to do with never fighting or never struggling but everything to do with being so connected at a very deep, real, and visceral level that almost nothing gets in the way. That's what makes emotional deep-diving possible for you to really know, be known, really love, and be loved, not for some polished picture of you but for who you are beneath.

It is for both of you, not just for them. It's a growth journey that you take together with your partner. That is why it lasts for years.

SECRET 7

THE ART OF LISTENING: COMMUNICATING FROM THE HEART

"Listening is an art that requires attention over talent, spirit over ego, others over self."

– Dean Jackson

Ever had a feeling that your partner does not really hear you, or perhaps there is even a time lag in what you want to convey? Sometimes, it can even be like they do not hear what you say. Frequently, you would like freely to express yourself without conveying too much of the other's perspective. The good news is that making your listening skills sharper can truly make your conversations richer!

The Art of Listening

This is a beautiful element that seeks its rightful place in the marvellous journey of love: the fine art of listening. Once again, it's easy to overlook this, especially as we are busy in lives filled with distractions and noise, that can drown out the subtle art of truly listening, so vital for forming genuine connections. It is the ability to listen and really hear one another that builds intimacy and a deep understanding of love.

Listening is not a passive activity; it becomes an engaging experience that, when done with purpose, transforms into a deep form of communication. This beautiful process has the potential to heal, nourish, and strengthen your relationship in amazing ways. It involves truly listening to your partner's words, understanding their emotions, and feeling the subtle undertones that lie beneath the surface. Every sigh, gesture, and pause is full of meaning, waiting to be discovered. This amazing skill will lead you to create a warm space for your partner so that they feel totally safe in expressing themselves.

I can proudly say that, as husband and wife, we are both patient listeners who value each other's opinions and emotional expressions. This has contributed to our rock-solid understanding and, I can proudly add, to our "No Fight" relationship. (Touch wood!)

Beyond Words

The journey begins with awareness. In our interactions, we are so occupied trying to think of what we are going to say that we become oblivious to hearing what the other person says. It becomes far too easy to just get lost in our thoughts and anxiously anticipate our moment to interject. Then, however, when we stop and, in reality, decide to listen instead, we introduce a delightfully new way of connectivity.

It is like peeling back the layers, revealing not only the words but also the deep-seated emotions and experiences that form them. Intentional listening is about commitment to understanding-it's more than just hearing the words; it's embracing the sea of emotions they carry with them.

Non-verbal cues, such as body language, eye movement, and even the tones in your partner's voice, constitute an important part of listening. Sometimes, subtle signs say more than any words. A furrowed brow may indicate concern and a warm smile may only be a reflection of being kind and understanding.

I request you to think deeply how often you go into a deep act of listening to all verbal and non-verbal cues of your partner. Because most of the time we do remain quite shallow on this aspect which can result in a communication gap. It may, at times, turn out to be one-way traffic if one of the partners becomes disinterested in what the other wants to say.

By truly paying attention to these gestures, you're engaging in a silent conversation that goes beyond words. This kind of attentive listening helps deepen your understanding of your partner, creating a lovely environment filled with empathy.

Openness and Honesty

Active listening is more than just a one-time effort; it's a beautiful journey that requires ongoing care and attention. Each day presents new opportunities to connect and express our feelings. However, our thoughts can sometimes get knotted—doubts and insecurities may creep in, obscuring our clarity. In such moments, we might misread our partner's intentions or respond in unforeseen ways. Yet, here's the encouraging part: it need not be complicated! When we engage in our conversations with openness and honesty, everything unfolds more easily, illuminating the genuine connection we hold.

It's not just listening to your loved one's words but also the development of self-awareness. It calls you to reflect on the reactions that make the conversation go around in circles. Consider this: when your partner opens up with their vulnerabilities, there may be an overwhelming urge to shield them through rationality. However, through this emotional truthfulness, you can cultivate a deeper relationship that brings you closer to your partner. This path requires "courage and perseverance"—the two most important qualities in order to have a serious conversation with empathy and consideration.

Friendly Atmosphere

Before having a serious conversation, it is helpful to take a few minutes to really centre yourself at the moment. Clear your mind of distractions and create a warm, inviting atmosphere. This might mean turning off the television, putting away your phones, or choosing a cosy nook in your home. A friendly environment would facilitate effective communication, in which attentive listening is cultivated and openness and vulnerability can be facilitated. In doing so, you are giving your partner an opportunity to freely express himself without any fear of interruption or even being misunderstood.

Bridging Communication Gap

Isn't it true that men and women are wired differently? We express our emotions uniquely and perceive them in distinct ways. Our responses to stressful situations and difficult times also vary. A man under stress might retreat into his shell for a while, while his partner may interpret this as him distancing himself. When she feels stressed, she tends to vent, seeking her partner's listening ear and empathy rather than immediate solutions, which men often feel compelled to provide as they try to fix things.

A romantic getaway effort, such as a fancy vacation by the male partner, may differ entirely from the concept of a series of small gestures, like daily compliments and little acts of kindness from the woman.

Connecting with validation

Being an active listener plays a pivotal role, and it all begins with the act of offering validation. When your partner shares a concern or expresses a feeling, resist the urge to immediately propose solutions or respond defensively; instead, take a moment to genuinely acknowledge their experience. A simple "I see how that made you feel" can change the course of the entire conversation. It communicates to your partner that their emotions are truly heard and valued. This approach encourages them to share even more, thereby strengthening the bond that exists between you both.

One of the essential features of proper listening is to recognise the importance of silence. More often than not, we think that silence is awkward- a gap that needs to be filled with irrelevant talk. However, in reality, silence can be a brilliant pause- an opportunity for reflection and deep understanding. You let your partner share his or her emotions in much deeper ways if you embrace those silences in your conversations.

At times, emotions become too overwhelming to be able to really listen. When emotions peak, there is a desire to step back or react without thought. It's then particularly helpful to focus on controlling those emotions. Take a breath and recall that listening is fundamentally about staying open to understanding, connecting with others, and building relationships.

Conclusion

The more you get into the art of listening, the more your relationship will bloom in ways you never thought possible. The more attuned you become to your partner, the deeper your emotional connection becomes. Love, after all, is more than grand gestures and eloquent phrases; it lies in the unflinching commitment to be present for each other, day after day, attentive and eager to listen.

Ultimately, learning to listen reveals a beautiful lesson in humility and vulnerability. It revolves around gently unravelling the layers of our ego and embracing the notion that true love transcends merely having answers; it lies in being sincerely present and authentically connected with one another. As you start this interesting journey of listening, remember that it is not a simple act; it is a deep commitment to fostering the beautiful, sometimes chaotic bond between two souls in love.

Effective communication is the pulse of every relationship and goes beyond even words because it actually feeds understanding and empathy. The dynamic inspires reflection while being a safe haven in which one can speak what one feels without the slightest hint of judgment.

As the remarkable author Leo Buscaglia so eloquently stated, **"Love is always there, but you must communicate it."** By cultivating our communication skills—by remaining present, posing open-ended questions, and wholeheartedly engaging in active listening—we forge connections that are not only meaningful but also transformative.

SECRET 8

LOVE LANGUAGES UNLOCKED: SECRETS TO DEEPER INTIMACY.

"Love a person the way they need to be loved, not the way you want to love. It's not about you. Love is selfless, not selfish."

– Tony Gaskins.

This is the relationship that remains an ageless dream in the world around us. We do not crave love but, instead, real intimacy- a connection that brings us together while being protective of individuality. This pursuit echoes throughout history- from epic stories of lovers in myth to romantic vows whispered under starry skies. What is it, however, that really deepens the intimacy in such relationships so they can withstand time? The answer lies in understanding the various ways we express and receive love.

Dr. Gary Chapman powerfully articulates in his book, "The 5 Love Languages", that every person has his or her unique way of expressing and receiving love. He calls this "love language." These languages can be used as a bridge to intimacy, which can enhance our romantic relationships and all our interpersonal relationships. Let's explore each one of these languages, their consequences, and how other languages may strengthen the bonds we build.

Words of Affirmation

Words hold immense power. They can uplift, motivate, and heal, but they also have the potential to inflict harm. For certain individuals, love is most deeply expressed through affirming words—compliments, gratitude, and encouragement. "Actions do not always convey more than words. If this is your partner's love language, they also need verbal affirmations of your love."

Consider all the moments you've exchanged compliments and expressions of appreciation with your partner. As I ponder this, I come to understand that I tend to hold back on my own compliments, and that seems rather unjust. Don't kind words or compliments lift your spirits? Absolutely! The annals of history are replete with timeless love stories that reveal how the expression of love through words can strengthen our bonds and illuminate our importance to one another.

Acts of Service

For some, love shows itself in acts such as cooking dinner, doing chores, or running errands, all of which are testimonies to love and devotion. It's not just the actions but the intentions that make them meaningful. When one person takes on responsibilities to make life easier for the other, it is a loud testimony of thoughtfulness.

Receiving Gifts

There's nothing quite like opening a gift that symbolises love. For those in love, gifts become effective symbols of love. The fact that the giver could think about the beloved person long enough to find and spend resources on a thoughtful gift speaks volumes.

Through history and ancient mythology, many examples demonstrate that material and spiritual endowments represent deep feelings and irrevocable commitment through tangible expressions of love. It is beyond the literal materialism but the thought and intention that defines the gesture.

Quality Time

Amidst the hustle and bustle of our busy lives, crafting meaningful moments in love is a beautiful expression. Quality time isn't just about occupying the same space; it is the giving of undivided attention to each other, getting absorbed in heart conversations, and actually being there in the moment. A remarkable difference exists between sitting on the couch, gazing at our phones, and having a real conversation that brings us closer.

By giving importance to these treasured moments in our lives, we can turn an ordinary life into a beautiful, interconnected adventure.

Physical Touch

Physical touch has a beautiful meaning in showing the depth of our care for one another. Simple gestures, such as hugging and holding hands, say volumes about love. Remember your first love—those unforgettable moments like intertwining fingers for the first time, embracing in that special hug, or sharing that tender first kiss; these are cherished memories that forge lasting connections and warmth within our hearts.

For those who value this language, physical intimacy fosters a sense of security and connection. Remember the famous "Jadu ki jhappi" in the Bollywood movie "Munnabhai MBBS"? We can all easily relate to the beautiful magic a warm embrace can create. It is said that hugs produce oxytocin in our bodies, which helps in emotional healing.

Warm hugs have always felt magical to me, ever since I was a child. I still cherish that wonderful feeling every time I share a hug with my wife and children. My wife has such a sweet way of keeping our connection alive by keeping one of my t-shirts close to her whenever I'm not around. It always brings me joy to know she does that!

Historically, emotions of love can be traced through the tapestry of colourful cultures. Just think about the lovely embrace passing between lovers in sonnets by Shakespeare, where every touch reveals deep emotion. Touch is a very natural way to provide warmth and comfort and to make a connection that feels just as deep emotionally as it does physically.

Shared Memories

Making shared memories is one of the most enjoyable ways to build our relationships! Whether travelling, discovering new hobbies, or just doing enjoyable things together, these can dramatically change the way we interact with one another. Not only do they bring us closer, but they also enrich our hearts with the joy of having happy times that strengthen the bond between people. In much the same way that old tribes came together for their celebration and storytelling, participating in such activities creates bonding through laughter, excitement, and growth.

Intellectual stimulation.

For many, love blossoms in the interesting conversations and exploration of new ideas. Books to read, philosophical questions to discuss, or diving into current events can develop deep emotional bonding that moves beyond the surface level. We create powerful connections through sharing our mutual intellectual curiosity that allows us to be genuinely seen and valued for our true selves.

Integrating Love Languages into Daily Life

Understanding love languages is half the journey; bringing them to life is what completes it. Here are some meaningful ways to weave these languages into the fabric of your relationship:

1. **Communicate Openly:** Engage in conversations about love languages with your partner. Comprehending one another's primary languages enriches your connection.
2. **Practice Daily Affirmations:** Establish a habit of sharing affirmations—be it through spoken words, handwritten notes, or texts.
3. **Acts of Service:** Anticipate your partner's needs and take the initiative to assist, whether it is preparing dinner or tidying up their workspace.
4. **Rituals of Gift-Giving:** Create small traditions around the act of giving, such as celebrating milestones with thoughtful, personalised gifts.
5. **Quality Time:** Ensure that quality time becomes a cornerstone of your schedules—plan night outs, weekends together, or even daily check-ins to connect with one another's feelings.
6. **Develop Physical Intimacy:** Cultivate those tender moments, whether it's walking hand in hand or cuddling up together on the couch.
7. **Be Here Now:** When with your partner, work to be fully present. Set aside distractions and engage in the here and now.
8. **Share Experiences Together:** Plan shared adventures, whether it's epic excursions like travelling or something as simple as trying a new café.

9. **Inspire Intellectual Interaction:** Participate in stimulating discussions, read books together, or attend seminars to promote intellectual growth and intimacy.

Conclusion

Exploring love languages unlocks a beautiful world of knowledge on the deeper connections we form with each other. It guides us through the waves and tides of relationships with greater compassion and understanding.

As Dr. Chapman states, **"Love is a choice you make every day."** By conscious acknowledgement and expression of the love languages of those we hold dear, we cultivate a distinct intimacy that not only fortifies our relationships but also enhances our lives.

Let us warmly welcome these beautiful languages as keys to open the world that is sometimes too big and overwhelming but, in its brilliance, is bursting with possibilities. Together, let's celebrate love as a great journey that will always teach us about ourselves, one another, and these great and precious bonds.

SECRET 9

MOMENTS THAT MATTER: THE POWER OF QUALITY TIME

"When you give someone your time, you are giving them a portion of your life that you'll never get back. Your time is your life. That is why the greatest gift you can give someone is your time."

– Rick Warren

For anyone approaching the end of life -thoughts tend to turn toward the relationships cherished, the laughter shared, and time passing far too quickly. "I wish I had spent more time with my family" is a common refrain many have uttered in the twilight of their lives. It is a poignant reminder that time is more than a commodity; it is the very heart of our relationships and the base upon which our happiness is built.

The Illusion

In a world of hustle and bustle, we often forget what truly matters. We fall into routines, distracted by responsibility and our relentless pursuit of success—a race without end that can often leave us feeling unfulfilled. I'm sure every person whether a working professional or a business entrepreneur busy in making a career or a successful venture will relate to this. Hence one requires to stop, lean into the present, and cherish each moment mindfully. For in the now lies fleeting beauty, and the manner in which we spend our time shapes our lives more deeply than any material good could.

Value of Time with Loved Ones

Imagine taking time to think about your schedule in a day for a moment. What is the frequency at which you find time for people in your life? We also keep aside quality time with our loved ones under the pretence of other commitments. The truth, however, is that tomorrow is not certain, and life has a way of surprising us in ways we cannot control. Children grow up quickly, blink, and they are off to forge their own paths, often consumed by their newfound independence and adult responsibilities. Moreover, as we age, our ability to enjoy those moments decreases, and what we once loved doing, such as playing games, hobbies, or just sharing laughter, may fade away into the background of nostalgia. Knowing this makes us take intentional steps today instead of waiting for tomorrow for meaningful connections.

I can say this with great conviction, having experienced where both of us as working professionals love to take out quality family time in terms of travelling for a holiday, a family dinner, visiting our grandparents, enjoying music together, painting on a canvas, Golf outing or even the small game of carrom is a great delight, absolutely rejuvenating after that hectic day at work.

Quality Over Quantity

It is so important that we break ourselves free from the misconception that more hours automatically imply better hours. The old adage we should internalise is quality above quantity. We can spend the best years of close, intimate physical presence and never feel emotionally close to another person; on the contrary, short moments of honest connection can shape our lives forever. Sometimes, it is in those unplanned events -that impromptu family dinner born of a sudden whim or an unexpected outdoor adventure-that the most joy is generated and lasting memories are formed.

Think about this: have you ever experienced a delightful joy in those little, fleeting moments—a true connection? conversation over steaming cups of coffee, a road trip overflowing with laughter, or a spontaneous dance in the kitchen—that evoked an unmistakable sense of joy? These moments can be much more rewarding than long periods spent in monotony or predictable routines. Life experiences are inherently vast and varied, and even in fleeting moments, we can embrace what it means to be alive, valued, and satisfied.

Consider the contrast between an extended family vacation brimming with distractions and a weekend well spent that fosters deeper connections.

In the latter scenario, the mere act of relishing each other's presence cultivates an environment where laughter, storytelling, and vulnerability can thrive. Whether it's a game night, preparing meals together, or exchanging tales beneath a starlit sky, these simple activities can turn ordinary evenings into treasured memories. These moments are the stories you share, the relationships you strengthen, and the legacy you create within your family.

In our pursuit of meaningful connections and the creation of cherished moments, it is crucial to foster an environment that focuses on engagement. Communication becomes very important here; it goes beyond the passing of time together and instead speaks to the importance of being present. In an age dominated by digital distractions, where screens can quickly hijack our attention, the act of actively listening to one another becomes an integral part of creating quality time.

Disconnect to Reconnect: Shared Experiences

Look at most of the families today. Everyone seems busy with their electronic gadgets, mostly mobile phones. I see even toddlers being made busy with the distraction of a mobile phone. Young teenagers are mostly immersed in social media, trying to catch up with the race of earning validation through likes on Instagram and Facebook.

We need to set technology aside during family gathering times—to put phones down, turn the TV off, and lose ourselves in conversation that actually means something. Ask people questions that make them open up; tell others what your hopes are for them, and get others to do likewise. That will create a culture of people feeling valued and heard. These moments can be so transforming in their nature, forging deep feelings of love and belonging. In the case of lunch or dinner, everybody must have freed themselves from other commitments and sit together for a good time.

Besides, time for shared experiences comes in many different forms. It is not necessarily big or elaborate; it can just find its way into the rhythm of life. Small, simple acts, such as a new tradition, sharing meals together, or even some sort of communal activity like gardening, can establish solid bonds. By taking the time to experience these collective experiences, your relationship deepens and grounds you in a comforting way.

It is equally important to note the deep power that silence can have. Sometimes, sitting together in silence can be very bonding, and this bonding is based on comfort and understanding. Whether watching a movie, taking a peaceful walk, or just existing in each other's presence, these moments prove that love does not necessarily need words; it can simply be felt.

The True Wealth and Legacy of Love

Remember, the actual wealth of life is not in accumulating wealth but in the quality of our relationships. When we place importance on our relationships, then time becomes a treasure feeding love, support, and togetherness. Cherish the beauty of the present moment as you journey through the intricacies of life, treasure it fully, and dive into every precious exchange.

And if, at the twilight of our years, we look back in the grand scheme of life, it is not all those accolades, all those promotions, or even all those possessions that matter the most. It will be the love we had for each other, the memories we forged, and the lives we touched—each one different in its own way. So choose deliberately to take time, be involved, and cherish these relationships that bring joy into your life. These are the moments that count.

As the American playwright Thornton Wilder once remarked, **"We can only be said to be alive in those moments when our hearts are conscious of our treasures."** The time shared with one another is indeed a treasure, a precious gift that enriches love and forges enduring memories.

Conclusion of Part 2

As we journey along the beautiful path of creating and developing relationships, we find the intimate secrets that truly make our relationships worthwhile. Friends, like family, bring love into our lives. Unconditional love gives us the deep satisfaction of giving, while emotional connections make our experiences more vivid. Open communication allows for a better understanding of one another, and personal boundaries help us to respect each other's individuality. Spending quality time together makes memories that we will cherish.

By embracing these elements, not only do we fortify the relationship but also cultivate lives that are rich in love, compassion, and meaningful connections. This chemistry of relationships makes every secret a vital piece in this intricate story of life, bolstering us through celebrations and challenges of life.

As we move on, let us embrace these truths and realise that love is not a destination in itself but a fluid and ever-changing journey. By dedicating ourselves to our connections and nurturing the cycle of love, we establish a robust foundation for relationships that can withstand time and enrich our lives in extraordinary ways.

PART 3

NAVIGATING RELATIONSHIPS AND EXPECTATIONS

Relationships can be a rollercoaster ride, with high points that thrill and low points that discourage, as well as twists you never expected. In this chapter, we will discuss the essential subtleties in navigating love and relationships based on the expectations we carry and the various influences that come our way. Let's have an open conversation about the intricacies of love, going into its paradoxes and embracing the imperfect nature of our experiences.

SECRET 10

THE FINE LINE: NAVIGATING BETWEEN EXPECTATIONS AND REALITY

"If you align expectations with reality, you will never be disappointed."

– Terrel Owens.

There's truly nothing quite like the magical wonder of young love! Standing on the brink of adulthood, gazing at the world through a blissful haze, love envelops you in a realm of infinite possibilities and surreal adventures. I vividly recall those years: the exhilarating thrill that surged through you when your eyes met someone who made your heart race. It felt almost as if you were soaring through the air, caught in a whirlwind of emotions where every love song resonates with your soul and every shared moment feels wonderfully enriching.

With stars sparkling in our eyes, we sweetly believe that love is the final destination, the ultimate triumph. But then, as if waking from an enchanting dream, you step into the colorful world of love, where the fairytale gradually dissolves like morning mist. You come to realize that love, as breathtaking as it is, carries a beautiful complexity: an enthralling blend of joy and challenge, excitement and effort. And it's evident that as captivating as it can be to fall in love, maintaining that love requires commitment, patience, and just a touch of talent!

The Expectation Gap

One of the first sobering lessons we learn in the realm of love is the gap between our expectations and reality. This gap can be huge and intimidating. Expectation is frequently fueled by the romantic and idealistic notion of love-a mixture of grand gestures, poetic declarations, and infinite passion. Reality, however, may be a mixed bag of shared responsibilities, mundane routines, occasional disagreements, but at the same time pleasant surprises.

Reflecting on my personal example I always had an expectation of marrying a sweet girl who would be a homemaker and not a strong working professional. I felt a working lady would not prioritise marriage and home over work. However, to my surprise, I fell in love with my wife, Ritu, knowing fully well that she was an army officer and a strong-willed lady. but she pleasantly amazed me with her love and devotion to me while displaying an immaculate work-life balance throughout our lives.

As the novelist Elizabeth Gilbert so poetically puts it, **"Marriage is like a long conversation, a conversation that gets deeper and truer as the years go on."** The above perspective gives one a reminder that love is not some collection of thrilling moments but has to be one that unfolds in a progression that requires engagement in a communication process, compromise, and confrontation with the truth about our partner and also about ourselves.

Infatuation to Commitment

In the early days of love, we tend to overlook small details that make it really special. The rush of infatuation sweeps us away in a delightful whirlwind, infusing the air with admiration and affection between partners. However, this enchanting phase is all too often built on very fragile ground—physical attraction and idealised views of each other. Time moves on, and reality quietly slips in, turning the initial thrill into emotions etched by our experiences.

As the glow of new love begins to dim down, couples start discovering each other's peculiarities and flaws. It is quite a lovely experience to appreciate someone from afar, but it becomes a different trip when one learns to like the characteristics that make an individual.

"Love doesn't have to be flawless; it simply needs to be true." This profound insight gently leads us through the tumultuous waves of affection, encouraging us to embrace our imperfections instead of pursuing unattainable ideals. Effort: The Bridge Over Troubled Waters

It was clear as we reflected on the successful relationships that it is all about the effort we put in. Love is not a feeling; it is an action, a daily commitment we decide to take together. This view inspires us to actively engage in our relationships. While we come across so many romantic quotes suggesting love is easy, they fail to remind us that effort is what makes love thrive.

Picture relationships as vibrant living entities requiring our attention and energy to truly thrive. Much like a plant that flourishes under the nourishing embrace of water and sunlight, love blossoms with the nurturing touch of care. Whether it's engaging in heartfelt conversations or being present for one another during life's highs and lows, the essence of a lasting relationship lies in our dedication to investing time and energy into each other. And bear in mind effort doesn't always manifest in grand gestures.

It is often the little mundane acts of kindness that truly count. Most couples enter their relationships with silent expectations, expecting their mates to know what they need and want. This silent construction of hope only sets a foundation for misunderstandings and resentments.

We need to be active in talking about our needs, desires, and fears and then let our partners get involved and respond accordingly. One of the most famous marital stability researchers, Dr. John Gottman, has observed: **"The secret to a long-lasting relationship is not finding someone who will meet all your needs, but finding someone who shares your values and can work with you to navigate life together."** This profound insight sums it up that communication serves as the foundation on which mutual understanding flourishes.

Changing Expectations with Time

As time goes on, expectations also evolve. Thus, one needs to thoughtfully reevaluate their goals for partnerships. At first, we all look forward to great romantic moments. However, in the course of life, when responsibilities accumulate, a person might find himself or herself focusing more on things such as building a home, raising kids, or perhaps achieving shared goals.

It is helpful then to take the flexible mentality in reflecting on this and allowing expectations to shift such that both partners grow together rather than resisting the change that life inevitably brings about. This does not at all mean settling for less; it instead shows that maturity in love is indeed a dynamic process that would require constant negotiation and calibration.

Gratitude as the Catalyst for Connection

One of the powerful ways to bridge the expectations-reality gap is through the cultivation of gratitude. Expressing gratefulness for each other ignites a positive feedback system, enhancing emotional connection and resilience. Recognising the sacrifices made and the small gestures made to make the relationship work itself can ignite warmth and add intimacy.

Being thankful does not really require much; one only has to note the little things and cherish them. Focusing on those good times helps boost relationships between partners, who make enough room for love to blossom, even when things seem hard.

Love is really about sticking together, trusting each other, and being brave enough to deal with the unknown without getting scared. Enjoy the ride together while figuring out that tricky balance between what we expect and what's real. Sometimes, it will take us in some surprising detours, but in those uncertain times is where we can really test our love, change it up, and make it even stronger.

Conclusion

Love is this delicate balance between expectation and reality. The romance of it all is beautiful, but the true beauty is in navigating life's complexity through intention, effort, and open dialogue. By embracing both the highs and lows, recognising our differences, and celebrating each moment, we nourish a love that not only endures life's trials but thrives within them.

Hey, let's remember that the best connections do not come from daydreams but from the choices we make every day. These choices, based on hard work, understanding, and appreciation, can bridge the gap between what we hope for and what's real, leading us to a closer bond that creates lasting love. Get ready for a long adventure of discovering each other since every step we take together paves the way to a more meaningful and satisfying relationship.

SECRET 11

LOVE'S PARADOX

"The paradox of love is that it can only be kept by giving it away."

– Richard Bach

"Love is a constant paradox: it demands closeness and distance, vulnerability and strength, freedom and commitment—all at the same time."

– Esther Perel

Love is one of those crazy mysteries of life that makes you want to dig deeper. It can lift you up to the highest heights of happiness, but it can also drag you down to some pretty dark places. The people we care most about can bring us our biggest smiles and also be the ones who hurt us the most.

This is what love does with the intermingling of happiness and pain, shaping our experiences in deep, sometimes conflicting ways. These contradictions make clear how love can be that great force for good but also a source of struggle. Love, at its core, is all about that deep sense of connection that brings belonging, fulfilment, and intimacy into our lives. When we fall in love, everything just seems different, right? The colours pop more, laughter feels way more joyful, and even the simplest stuff feels like magic. This super exciting time releases a bunch of endorphins, making us feel like love is this awesome, positive thing—kind of like a cure that heals our wounds and makes those lonely feelings disappear. Yet, the ones who have loved fully, with heart and soul, know how this beautiful state can change in a surprising way. The same person who brings so much joy to our hearts at certain times can cause heart-wrenching pain as well.

The Paradox of Love: A Complex Landscape

Let us explore some of these paradoxes: joy vs pain, transactional vs. transformational, healer vs. destroyer, and the capacity of both achievement and despair fostered in the same relationship.

The Joy and Pain of Love

To get this paradox, let's really soak in the joy love brings. At first, love is like a fairytale, all about passion, chemistry, and dreaming big together. Hanging out with someone you love is such a special gift; every look feels like it has its own vibe. This bond fills us up with happiness—just think of all the laughter, a cosy hug, or just chilling together.

In love, we find companionship. Daily struggles feel lighter when shared. Motivated by love, one becomes better, inspires growth and nurtures dreams. It fuels creativity and kindness that helps in acts of service or support that add meaning and beauty to the life experience of connection.

Love brings pain with it as closely tied to its sweetness-the pain is an essential factor in our emotional journey. The closeness of love makes us open and vulnerable, sharing hearts and unveiling fears, desires, and dreams. This blend of emotions is beautiful but risky. When trust falters or expectations go unmet, disappointment, betrayal, and loss can hurt, leaving emotional scars. Literature reflects this heartache, with tragic heroes experiencing profound loss, like Romeo and Juliet, illustrating love's potential for grief. Love ignites passion but can also result in emptiness when lost. The person we love most can also inflict deep hurt. The phrase "this is going to hurt" resonates in relationships, where misunderstandings or unmet needs can create rifts, jeopardising the bond that once united them.

Transactional vs. Transformational Love

At its surface, love can sometimes appear transactional—a give-and-take dynamic where affection is exchanged for specific benefits or needs. In such arrangements, individuals may seek validation, security, or companionship based on what the other offers rather than genuine emotional connection. This kind of love makes people dependent or entitled since they're always measuring what they get out of the relationship. For example, some people will hang around not just for love but also for money, status, or fitting in with others.

But you know, love can become so much more than just what you give and receive. It can help you grow in ways that are much deeper than that. It's like, think about couples who are focused on lifting each other up and supporting each other's dreams. They are teammates in building their future, and they're there to cheer each other on too.

Love doesn't see any limits or barriers. It breaks through all kinds of walls to get where it needs to go. This cool part of love shows how much change can happen when two people decide to grow together.

Healer vs. Destroyer

Probably, healing ability is the most praised aspect of love. Love can comfort us in our hour of grief, help us pass through hardships, and restore our faith in human nature. Being loved gives us a sense of comfort, which leads to healing of the mind and heart. In this regard, love becomes a balm for wounds, a place of refuge where people are valued and understood.

Reflecting on my experience with a significant life-threatening accident, I truly felt the healing power of love of my family, parents and all those who care for me. Even during the toughest emotional times, it's the love from those dear to you that gives you the strength to rise above the pain of loss.

However, love can also be incredibly destructive. When things go awry, it may lead to obsession, jealousy, or control. These intense emotions can drive individuals to commit extreme negative acts.

Romantic relationships often have destructive potential. Passion and possessiveness can create emotional upheaval. Love can become debilitating, leading to dependency that strips away individuality and autonomy. Many historical narratives illuminate the dual nature of love; it has the power to heal, yet can also result in heartbreak and chaos if not approached with mindfulness and self-awareness.

Creator of Achievers vs. Source of Despair

Well, love really makes people do some incredible stuff. With support, encouragement, and a partner believing no matter what, it lights a fire under your ambitions and gives you a sense of purpose that fuels both personal and work successes. In good relationships, love is like this spark that motivates people to take risks, chase their dreams, and try for the best.

But, as we know, love can totally create a weird cycle of sadness, too. Just one bad relationship can hold someone back from really shining. When love gets all conditional—like when it's filled with manipulation, letdowns, or needs that never get met—it can make people feel unworthy, confused, and even super down. The expectations we put on our partners can start to feel like a heavyweight, turning life into a stressful race instead of something fulfilling.

Take Vincent van Gogh, for instance. His ardent passion for art was simultaneously a wellspring for his greatest work and the deepest cause for his torment. Brilliant as he was, his personal demons defeated him; he felt terribly lonely and desperate. So, this guy said, "I put my heart and soul into my work and have lost my mind in the process." It kind of shows how love—whether it's for art or someone special—can really highlight both the amazing things we can do and the tough phase we go through.

The Fine Line Between Love and Dependency

Love is pretty amazing, right? But it can sometimes get a bit tangled up with dependency. It really feeds our need to connect and belong, making those bonds that give us comfort and happiness. But then again, those tight connections can make us forget who we really are. When we depend too much on each other for emotional support or validation, it can end up slowing down our personal growth.

It is quite hard to differentiate between being too dependent and genuinely caring for each other when two people get really close. The vibe of the relationship may change from helping each other grow to a point where both partners just hang on to each other, which makes it hard for either of them to thrive solo. This is such a mind-bender: love, which is all about connecting with others, can sometimes mess up our path to being the best versions of ourselves accidentally.

Gifts of Love and the Costs of Attachment

Lastly, love represents the paradox of gifts and costs. Loving relationships may be laden with joy, companionship, and deep understanding; meanwhile, they require sacrifice and compromise. Giving love implies vulnerability and possible hurt as well as loss. A paradox in its very concept, it shows how inherently we take risks to reap the opportunity of having experiences of deep joy.

The tricky part is realising that every relationship has its costs—like time, energy, emotional investment, or compromise—but it's actually those same costs that make our shared experiences so valuable.

Figuring Out the Tricky Part

Navigating the complexities of love actually invites us to embrace both wisdom and resilience. When one starts to realise that joy travels hand in hand with pain, there is a relationship deepening and a more profound understanding of oneself. Accepting that beautiful duality can sometimes ground one and help in celebrating highs while finding lessons from lows in love.

Cultivating emotional intelligence is a great way to enrich our journey. It means tuning into our feelings and also to our partners; hence, open and constructive communication can be fostered. Instead of withdrawing into silence when hurt or disappointed, we have the beautiful opportunity to share our feelings. Acknowledging the pain is the first step towards healing, and the discussion of grievances can bring about solutions that strengthen rather than unravel our connection.

One of the beautiful lessons we gather from the Bhagavad Gita is the importance of maintaining equanimity and balance at all times, even in the face of life's ups and downs. Only then can we truly appreciate the fleeting nature of love's volatile outcomes in comparison to the serenity that comes from an enduring essence of love.

Additionally, this reminds us that learning from the past better enables us to face future challenges. Looking back at our mistakes, we learn valuable insights about behaviours we can change. Forgiveness—towards each other and towards ourselves—transforms our pain into a source of strength and healing.

The Promise of Love

As we know, even with all the ups and downs, the crazy ride of love is totally worth it. Being able to love deeply, along with all the stuff that comes with it, really shows off our humanity in such an amazing way. The happiness we get from loving relationships usually beats out any hurt we might deal with; it's through love that we grow and learn more about ourselves and our connections with others.

Ultimately, such a journey of love teaches us crucial truths about ourselves. We learn resilience and vulnerability, authenticity and compassion. Through this journey, we come to understand the elements of happiness and sorrow in life that have to be embraced as essential parts of a fulfilled life in which we can feel deeply and connect with someone else on a similar plane. It's really this journey that really helps us feel the profound ability of love, lifting our spirits and profoundly changing what it means to be human.

Conclusion

Love's paradoxes totally highlight how complicated it is - like it can really boost our lives and also throw some challenges our way at the same time. The moment we accept that love has this two-sided nature, we can handle our relationships with a bit more wisdom, understanding, and kindness. As we go through all the ups and downs of love, we end up finding a whole range of experiences - each one teaching us important stuff about ourselves and how we connect with other people.

Realising these contradictions helps us build stronger and healthier relationships. We start to get that love isn't just something you feel and do nothing about; it's this ever-changing thing that needs our attention and effort. In the end, love is a deep journey that takes us through both the good times and the bad, making a space full of awesome chances for growth, understanding, and change.

SECRET 12

BEYOND INFLUENCES: CHARTING YOUR OWN COURSE IN LOVE

"Love is not about following someone else's map; it's about creating a journey together that feels right for both of you."

– Unknown

Love is often seen as a beautiful, transcendent journey between two people. It forms a deep connection, blossoming through mutual understanding and openness. However, anyone who has experienced love knows this ideal bond isn't isolated. We live in a world influenced by external factors—our families, friends, social norms, and even the ever-present flow of social media—that can profoundly affect our close relationships.

The Family Factor: Support or Strain?

Family is often the first level of influence we interact with. The family created our thoughts about relationships and values and taught us what to expect from each other. They pass down the wisdom they have gained from experience and even steady our love lives sometimes. They always want the best for us, after all. However, this influence can sometimes be a double-edged sword.

On the positive side, family can provide essential guidance in navigating the complexities of romantic relationships. A supportive family might offer wisdom that helps you identify red flags or encourages open communication with your partner. They can help you see things differently, fostering a well-rounded view of your relationship.

On the other hand, familial influence can also be sometime overbearing, transforming into unwarranted interference that can suffocate a couple's bond. Family members are likely to question your choices of relationships, speak out of turn about your choices and relationship, and they may even make comments that suggest your partner is not good enough for you.

This kind of intrusion may create confusion, resentment and distance between partners. At this point, boundaries become vital. One must respect family relationships but establishing a boundary that first gives importance to your partnership and respects the sanctity of that relationship is equally important.

Family therapist and author Harriet Lerner says,**"In any marriage, the husband and wife are expected to be entirely devoted to each other. Yet their success often hinges on their ability to manage the expectations of their extended families."**

Therefore, there has to a delicate balance between familial loyalty and nurturing your romantic love.

The Role of Friends: Laughter and Loyalty or Misguidance?

Like a good family, friends have this fantastic way of moulding your relationships. They become a trusted confidant during the hard times, the ones that make life colourful by filling our lives with laughter and joy. Spending time with friends in the evening brings such warmth and lightness, transforming life's daily burdens into shared moments of support and happiness.

Sometimes, friends who brighten our days may overstep and share opinions that don't quite mirror our unique relationships. For instance, they might say that one should leave the partner during difficult times, and they do not know the depth and context of that commitment. In such moments, they might unknowingly plant seeds of doubt that influence the trust and communication we maintain in our partnerships.

Lovely also is the acknowledgement of the types of friendships we cultivate in our existence. Some are always available to cheer us on, encouraging us to love more radically with open hearts, whereas others approach love with at least a bit of scepticism that can nudge us slightly off course.

Societal Spotlight: Cultural Expectations and Norms

Societal norms are very influential in our love lives, most of the time dictating expectations that have to be met. Such norms vary dramatically from place to place, as well as cultural background and social context.

Take India for example. In most Asian countries, family and social customs place a high emphasis on tradition and family-oriented considerations as a basis for relationships; arranged marriages are a norm, and even relationships are often under the scrutiny of extended families and the community. Societal expectations may, at times, be set above individual desires, resulting in clashes between individual happiness and cultural obligations. In a more liberal society, more is made of individual fulfilment and personal choice, leading to a more open relationship with multiple definitions of commitment. What one culture finds acceptable might be seen as rather negative in another. That knowledge helps individuals to be better partners to themselves in understanding how to engage with societal norms and personal desires.

The Social Media Mirage: The Illusion of Perfection

Social media introduces an entirely new layer of influences within the hyper-connected world. Platforms like Instagram, Facebook, and TikTok are all filled with carefully curated moments of seemingly perfect lives and, therefore, can produce an illusion of success and happiness that blurs our reality.

We scroll down posts full of picture-perfect couples travelling the world, celebrating milestone anniversaries, or sharing lavish public displays of affection and, not even realising it, start comparing our relationships to those unrealistic standards. The results can be damaging: self-doubt, dissatisfaction, and the conviction that our love in some way compares poorly.

Furthermore, the instant gratification era also makes people question their commitment, seeking a boost from likes and comments, which will eventually blur the line of genuine connection. Dr. Jean Twenge, a psychologist and author, affirms, **"Social media may offer a sense of connection, but it can also amplify feelings of isolation and inadequacy."** This is the paradox: we are more connected than ever, yet we feel increasingly distant from real intimacy.

Rooted in Values

Today, with the world being in love, building a solid foundation of values, trust, and commitment is essential. Outside pressures require couples to be self-aware, communicate openly, and confidently connect in their relationship.

Begin with a few minutes of reciting your core values as individuals and as a couple. What are the beliefs and principles that really guide your love? Are you placing any boundaries around family influence, friends' opinions, or societal expectations? These heart-centred conversations begin with shared understanding and ensure that both parties align with their vision of love.

Open communication can really anchor you during external challenges. Checking in with each other about how the relationship is going, sharing feelings, and airing concerns strengthens the bond between you two. This type of open dialogue creates an area for tackling potential issues before they become bigger problems and reinforces a genuine sense of partnership flowing between you two.

Finding Balance: Conformity vs. Individuality

The interplay between one's own desires and those of society adds a rich layer of complexity to their relationships. It is most important to be true to oneself, but sometimes embracing social norms can help make familial expectations and interactions with society a little easier to accept.

Finding that sweet balance is key here—what can we honour in societal expectations, and where do we carve some space for what makes our relationship unique? For example, the blending of traditions or the respect for expectations with which we align and can yet celebrate individuality and preferences could add richness to the quality of our relationships.

This duality requires reflection and intentional action toward embracing the social norms yet holding onto oneself. It's that thin line between opening up to feedback yet standing firm in the direction of your love.

As we wind our way through the twists and turns of love, it is but a normal thing to experience all those influences of family, friends, society, and, not least, social media. All these external agents may mould and shape your experiences, but they would never define what your relationships were all about. Knowing their effects would make us navigate through love with a better view of when to open ourselves to outside perspectives and how much to hold onto what we believe in.

The secret to growing a love that thrives despite the pressures of outside influences is staying grounded in your values, communicating openly, and mutually trusting and understanding each other.

By dealing with these influences proactively, we can light the way to lasting love, not only celebrating the connections that enhance our lives but also the bond we share with each other. Embrace this journey—although outside factors will influence our experiences, it is the heart of our love that drives us onward.

Key Takeaways

- Understand your own Love language and needs.
- Don't rely only on family and friends for advice.
- Celebrate your unique qualities as a couple.
- Setting healthy boundaries is crucial to balance family loyalty with romantic partnership.
- Strike a balance between respecting societal norms and personal desires.
- Genuine connections require focusing on real-life interactions rather than online validation.
- Find Balance Between Conformity and Individuality.
- Stay grounded in mutual trust and shared values.

SECRET 13

BEAUTIFULLY IMPERFECT: EMBRACING FLAWS IN YOURSELF AND OTHERS

"Nobody is perfect; nobody is correct. In the end, affection is always greater than perfection. "

– Unknown.

"True love is not about perfection; it is hidden in flaws, in deep emotional connection, and in being vulnerable together."

– Unknown.

Let's chat about imperfection. "Why do we feel like we have to be perfect?" you might wonder. In a world that makes such a big deal out of this ideal love and relationship thing, it's super easy to forget that every single person—us, too—has their own flaws.

In a world flooded with all those perfect pics—like flawless bodies, gorgeous homes, and picture-perfect relationships—it's totally easy to feel swamped. Social media bombards us with messages about how things "should" look, and we end up yearning for an impossible ideal. The beauty of human existence is beautifully messy. We are imperfect creatures, and life is very complex, nuanced, and inconsistent. Nobody is perfect, and no relationship could ever be perfect. You have to find the forever love with all the flaws in you and in them.

The Myth of Perfection

You know, perfection is this big, kind of tricky idea. Society tells us we should aim for this ideal—whether it's how we look, our bank accounts, or how chill we are emotionally. But honestly, these ideals can create crazy expectations that mess with how we see love and affection. Like Anne Lamott once said, **"Perfectionism is the voice of the oppressor."** While we're out here chasing a perfect life, we might totally miss out on the beauty in our quirks and imperfections.

Realising that people are naturally flawed frees us from the chains of perfectionism. Everyone's got their own story, background, and experiences that make them who they are.

Shifting our mindset from chasing perfection to accepting authenticity can totally change how we love.

Redefining Beauty: It's More Than Just Looks

You know, one of the biggest ways we see imperfection is in how we look. Society has all these crazy ideas about what's "beautiful," mostly just about how you look on the outside. Honestly, though, these ideas mess with our idea of beauty; what one culture loves, another might not even care about. And so we end up running after this ever-changing, often impossible ideal.

In romantic relationships, getting too caught up in how someone looks can totally hide the more important stuff. Think about a partner who might not match what everyone says is beautiful but really shows kindness, integrity, and warmth. Those kinds of traits build a deep, loving bond. A genuinely nice person is way more valuable than just a pretty face.

As poet Kahlil Gibran beautifully captured in his work "The Prophet", "**Beauty is not in the face; beauty is a light in the heart.**" This perspective shifts our focus from external attributes to emotional resonance. A loving partner who warms our soul is infinitely more valuable than a copy of a magazine cover model.

Financial Imperfection: Valuing Character Over Wealth

Something else related to imperfection comes up when discussing financial stability. We imagine the ideal partner as financially stable, educated, and very driven. Okay, financial stability is great, but it shouldn't take over the more significant qualities that make a good partner. Just imagine having someone who may not have much money but is honest, caring, and genuinely focused on personal growth.

Relationships that are only about money cannot have that emotional bond. Well, yes, cash might remove some stress, but it will never replace love, support, and good morals. A partner who chases after their dreams, appreciates what is truly important rather than glitz and glamour, and lifts you up when you are at your lowest can totally make your life a better one in ways that no amount of cash can.

Emotion with Compassion

Every relationship comes with its own set of emotional flaws. Maybe one partner is super sensitive or has dealt with a lot of emotional ups and downs before. It might seem like a downside at first, but being emotionally vulnerable can actually be a strength, too. Vulnerability helps create honesty and openness between partners, making it a comfortable environment for connecting and growing together.

People usually think of emotions as a weakness. But honestly, emotions are not really good or bad; they're just human. When people share their emotions, that usually leads to stronger relationships and helps both partners empathise and get along.

This calls for developing patience and compassion for one another. Acknowledge that having different emotional reactions is a part of living with someone else. When your partner cannot find the words to express his or her emotions, remember that his or her emotional state does not lessen your relationship. Understanding with compassion creates a relationship where both partners can discuss the intricacies of love without fear of judgment.

The Power of Intentions

It is about intentions that tie us together in romance. Honestly, it's not about being perfect; it's really about being genuine in what we do. When we are figuring out our relationships, recognising the good vibes and positive intentions popping up despite the flaws can really strengthen our connections.

"A person who may not be perfect but has good intentions is always better than someone who appears perfect but harbours bad intentions towards you."

Sometimes, they struggle to show love in difficult times, misunderstand, or get defensive because of fear. Such mistakes are all human. But if you can see the love and good intentions underneath, then it can really help both of you recover from such misunderstandings and connect better with each other in more empathetic ways.

Consider the approach used in Cognitive Behavioural Therapy (CBT), which focuses on separating behaviours from the individual. By knowing that a bad action doesn't define a person's character, we can facilitate growth while promoting acceptance. This view can reduce tension and open up for reconciliation, making imperfection a chance for a deeper connection.

Changing Perspectives: Acceptance Over Judgment

It is then that, upon these shortcomings, the very act of perspective can create transformation. Don't focus on the imperfections your partner seems to have. Encourage acceptance of the beauty within the chaos.

Acceptance fosters an open-hearted attitude toward love. It is letting go of the idea that your partner is the idealised version of themselves and embracing them for who they are. Imperfections lead to a deeper appreciation for the person beside us; they invite us to explore the depths of their character and understand the experiences that have shaped them.

When we accept ourselves, we also extend grace to our partners. This nurturing atmosphere fosters trust, commitment, and a sense of belonging that enriches the emotional landscape of your relationship.

Growing through imperfection

Acknowledging mistakes makes room for development in personal and relationship lives. When couples admit the wrongs they commit, space is created for honest talk about aspirations and desires. It makes them much more responsible, and this becomes the emotional base of relationships.

Consider a couple who has weaknesses. One of them may want to improve in being more responsible about finances, while the other wants to improve communication. Expressing weaknesses will allow them to work together to improve rather than hide behind their shortcomings. Teamwork can strengthen companionship and strengthen mutual respect.

Dealing with flaws together builds up resilience. Couples who tackle problems side by side create a shared story filled with lessons, progress, and wins over tough times. This kind of growth really tightens their connection, giving them a solid base as they keep figuring out the crazy ups and downs of life.

Conclusion: Embracing the Journey of Love

It is not finding one person who checks all the boxes but loving all the messiness and all the quirks in another human being. Accepting flaws and those of our counterparts will lead us into a much more profound journey of real closeness.

Accepting our common human flaws helps develop qualities such as compassion, patience, and resilience. Love is a journey that is a colourful mix of emotions, challenges, and victories shaped by the unique individuals who share their lives together. In accepting flaws in ourselves and our partners, we open up spaces for authenticity, vulnerability, and deeper connections in relationships.

Hey, let's celebrate how rich our human experiences are and show love in all its messy beauty. When we believe in our imperfections, it lets us experience a deeper and more lasting love that grows not from chasing perfection but from the awesome chaos of just being human.

It is in the acknowledgement of our little quirks that we open the door to real connections, where being honest matters more than chasing after some perfect idea. And loving genuinely becomes flourishing when we embrace our specific flaws; we go beyond the amazing moments and beautiful chaos of human existence.

SECRET 14

SPACE TO GROW: BALANCING INDEPENDENCE AND TOGETHERNESS

"Let there be spaces in your togetherness, and let the winds of the heavens dance between you."

– Khalil Gibran

"The best relationships are the ones where you can be deeply connected, yet still feel free to be yourself."

– Unknown

Isn't it just great to feel this bond, basking in the warmth of shared moments and emotional closeness? Yet, at the same time, we really cherish our independence—loving freedom to chase our dreams and figure out who we are. So, here is a big question: can we have independence and togetherness without getting in each other's way, or does one end up messing with the other?

Harmony of Connection and Individuality

To really get into what makes relationships last, we got to recognise this important thing: love grows when both people are pushed to be their own selves. Romantic love isn't about giving up who you are; it should light a fire that drives your own paths. A true partnership is all about teaming up—it's that kind of relationship where each person lifts up the other's dreams and goals without worrying about losing themselves in it.

Every relationship comes with its set of expectations—the dreams and ideas we build while figuring things out together. However, for a relationship to be healthy, both persons must feel good about themselves first so that they can chase their own goals yet still enjoy time together. Finding that sweet spot allows love to grow rather than shrink, keeping both independence and connection alive.

Ecosystem of a Thriving Relationship

Think of a relationship that's as cool and diverse as nature! Just like every species plays a part in keeping the ecosystem alive, your own quirks really add to your partnership. When your partner's off chasing new career goals, getting into a hobby, or hanging out with friends, don't see it as something to worry about; it's just part of how you both grow together.

Think about it: when a partner feels restricted, it is just like a flower that can't bloom. The partner's dreams are much like a budding blossom that seeks sunlight to bloom.

Just remember, though you're going into the great journey of love, sometimes growing means giving each other a little space to explore yourselves. For one of you to really shine, it's super important for the other to support that journey. So, if your partner wants to hang out with friends for the weekend, try to feel happy about it instead of anxious; just embrace it! Their fun times with others can only make your connection even stronger!

Freedom vs. Neglect: Re-Defining Time Away

Imagine this: a husband having an awesome night out with his buddies, just soaking in the laughter and good vibes. Frankly speaking, that should not be seen as him ignoring his relationship. It's rather that he's taking some space, which helps him return all revved up and ready to rock their partnership. Similarly, when a wife is pursuing her dreams—is it attending a workshop or diving into a challenging project, or just having one of those relaxing girls' days out—she ought to feel supported by the other half. Recognizing that her passions contribute toward her personal growth helps instil a loving atmosphere born out of mutual respect.

Empowering your partner

In many households, women as homemakers indeed represent the warmth of unconditional love. They completely manage the house, take care of the kids, and balance a million tasks—often pushing their own aspirations and dreams to the back burner. Even when they have done all that hard work and emotional effort, they might end up feeling undervalued and overlooked, which can be really discouraging for the positive vibes. It is extremely important to uplift these amazing women by giving them opportunities for education and skills building, encouraging them to dive into their hobbies and passions. By creating a space that appreciates their unique talents and dreams, we not only celebrate what they bring to the table but also make our community's vibe even better.

The key thing is visibility—to really see each other in a loving relationship as being unique people. Rather than being fearful of time away, use those times to celebrate. When you start respecting the independence of another, you end up having a stronger connection.

Dealing with Insecurities: Having Each Other's Backs

But that does not mean independence comes without its challenges. Managing a relationship while giving room for growth can bring up feelings of jealousy, insecurity, or fear of abandonment. It is important to confront these emotions with open dialogue. Recognising and discussing feelings can turn what might be obstacles into chances to deepen trust and understanding.

When your partner talks about wanting to go their own way, it doesn't mean they're rejecting the relationship; it's more like they're inviting you to be part of their journey. Chatting about each other's dreams really helps you both feel connected and have a common purpose. You could ask stuff like, "What's the most exciting thing about this opportunity for you?" or "How can I help you reach this goal?"

That way, you assure them of their hopes and strengthen the relationship that both of you share.

A healthy relationship really thrives when you encourage each other. Just like in nature, where plants are all about competing for sunlight, your relationship gets stronger when you root for each other's growth. Make sure to celebrate your partner's little wins—like landing a promotion, picking up a new skill, or hitting a personal goal. When you're both out there cheering each other on, it doesn't just make your bond better; it also boosts your own self-esteem.

Redefining Togetherness and Shared Growth

Hey, let's just take a second to appreciate how cool it is to redefine "togetherness." Being together doesn't always mean doing everything at the same time; sometimes it's about rooting for your partner while they go off and do their own thing. This can totally change our perspective. Instead of seeing time apart as a bad thing, let's view it as a super important step to building an even stronger bond. When you think about symbiosis, it's pretty cool how balanced things can be. Healthy relationships are like two trees standing close by—supporting each other but also taking care of their own roots. When both people feel free to grow, the whole relationship just flourishes.

Imagine a partnership where you're celebrating each other's wins like they're both of yours. As they shine brighter, their bond grows richer and deeper, something special in its own ways.

It's important to understand that growth comes in many forms. It is not only a matter of physical distance, but emotional growth, intellectual pursuits, and spiritual explorations are also essential parts of the process. Asking your partner to explore activities that make them feel complete does not mean they're drifting away; it's a sign that both of you can grow together with support and nurturing.

You know, independence really shows how mature a relationship can be. When someone sticks to their own dreams and is so happy cheering on his partner's wins, that shows they have emotional smarts and strength. It is not about losing oneself, but it is more about appreciating those special things that make your relationship amazing together.

Keeping a love that lasts is really about making a spot where you can both be independent and still enjoy being together. It's awesome to give each other space to grow, totally cheer on your partner's dreams, and keep that open chat going that respects both of your individual quirks and your bond. Real love grows from a partnership that's all about trust, support, and really believing in what each other can achieve.

By weaving independence into the heart of your relationship, you cultivate a rich environment for lasting intimacy-one where love is enriched by the special qualities each partner brings. In this nurturing space, love goes beyond the everyday, blossoming into something truly extraordinary, ensuring that both partners flourish not just together but also as unique individuals on an exciting journey of continuous growth.

Boundaries are very important for keeping love alive. Of course, being together brings you close, but giving each other space helps keep that independent vibe going. Finding the right mix of both is key to not feeling trapped or bitter. In love, it's all about remembering that when you grow as individuals, it just makes your shared moments even better and strengthens your bond.

When couples respect each other's boundaries, it lets their love bloom while still staying true to themselves.

Conclusion of Part 3

We uncover valuable knowledge as we make our journey through the twists and turns of relationships and expectations. Careful wishes open us up to realistic and satisfying relationships while recognising that love operates in paradox and allows one to navigate all the ins and outs between joy and pain. If we take into account influences from elsewhere, we'll be sure to maintain authentic relationships, and finally, imperfection frees us from the pressures of unrealistic expectations.

When it comes to this thing called love, just prepare for the unexpected, get accustomed to the quirks, and just hold fast to that promise of love and honour, both toward yourself and your partner. Real magic isn't perfection; it's how love changes and grows. So, let's keep moving forward, embracing this wild ride of love in all its wonderfully messy glory!

PART 4

TRUST, CONFLICT RESOLUTION AND HEALING

Trust is the cornerstone of any relationship. Imagine your love life as a house you built with care. Trust is the solid ground it's standing on; if that's not there, everything starts to tip over and fall apart. In this chapter, we'll delve into how to build trust, deal with conflicts, and embrace the powerful process of forgiveness and healing. Get ready —this is where the real magic of relationships happens!

SECRET 15

BUILDING BRIDGES: THE FOUNDATIONS OF TRUST AND COMMITMENT

"Trust takes years to build, seconds to break, and forever to repair."

– Unknown

When it comes to love, trust and commitment are huge deals. They are the backbone of a good relationship, giving you a solid base to handle life's ups and downs. But trust can be pretty delicate; it can get broken easily by mix-ups, betrayals, or just the little mistakes we all make as human beings. Building trust and commitment is not merely the act of saying "I love you." It is an ongoing process that requires effort, intention, and introspection.

The Nature of Trust: A Delicate Balance

Trust is such a complicated thing, right? It's that tricky little quality that makes you feel secure when opening up about your fears, knowing that your partner is listening and really gets you. Trust lifts us up and helps us reach those high emotional peaks while also providing that safety net when we stumble. But, like in any solid relationship, trust has to be earned. You can't just hand it out.

Start with honesty and transparency to build trust. It is not about revealing secrets but opening up about emotions, needs, and intentions. That requires a degree of vulnerability most people fear and are afraid of, and that they will judge or reject them. In real intimacy, however, openness thrives. When you share what's on your mind and how you feel, you are not only letting your partner into your inner world but also paving the way for understanding and respect between you two.

Think about it: a relationship really grows from all of those little, kind of boring moments that add up and build trust. It is not only the big, romantic moves; it's just recognising each other in little things and sticking to your word that really matters. You chat with your mate, keep your promises or listen without judgment. There, you're putting bricks into the foundation of building trust.

The Slow Build: Patience in Fortifying Relationships

Trust is a marathon and not a sprint. Years are needed to build, but only seconds to break. Most importantly, though, trust can be broken and fixed; it will just take a long time and, above all, conscious effort on both parts.

You know that old adage about trust being like a bank account? Well, it is totally true. Every good interaction adds a little bit of cash into that account, but when something goes wrong, it feels like withdrawal. Like if your partner misses an important event or is distant for a while, it's definitely a withdrawal. But if they keep coming around, giving you emotional support, and talking things out, that balance just keeps getting better!

In this sense, recognising the importance of consistency is crucial. Each promise kept adds to the account, while each disappointment diminishes it. Over time, those little moments become significant: a phone call when you're running late, an encouraging text during a tough day, or simply a listening ear. Each of these gestures becomes a building block—laying the foundation for a trust that can withstand life's weathers.

Facing Challenges Together

Challenges in relationships can occur. Life is not going to always be easy; it'll throw some rough patches that really test your connection. In some ways, how you navigate through those times can make all the difference in the amount of trust between you two. Those tough moments are chances for partners to show the amount of commitment they have to each other and to the relationship.

For instance, conflict is viewed as something bad; one should always avoid it. But at the same time, it can be a turning point, an opportunity for better understanding and growth. How you ride through these storms defines your relationship. You should confront disagreements together, not retreating into corners. Not being defensive may help you create an atmosphere where both of you can feel safe in expressing how you feel.

Also, when things get rough, reaching out to each other emotionally can really help build trust and keep things transparent. Are you both on the same wavelength? Getting where each other is coming from during tough times can boost trust a ton. As Brené Brown says, **"Vulnerability is the birthplace of innovation, creativity, and change."**

Trust grows in those vulnerable moments, where both partners feel safe sharing their fears and hopes.

The Commitment Factor

Trust is like the base that would get you close to the person. Commitment, on the other hand, is a bit like glue. It's not just about saying you are going to do something, but it's actually the choice of putting effort into the relationship every single day. It means being there for your partner, accepting their quirks and flaws, and being ready to tackle any issues that come your way together.

One big part of commitment is being consistent. You can say, "I love you," a million times, but it's really what you do that proves you mean it. Showing up—whether it's emotionally, physically, or mentally—when it counts is what really shows you're committed. This could be anything from going to important events to just hanging out during chill times.

You know, relationships have always been about the idea that commitment really means something. Just look at all the marriage rituals people have everywhere—whether it's super serious vows or just casual promises. Those things are like a sign of a stronger connection, showing that you're both in this for the long run.

As Abraham Lincoln said, "Commitment is what transforms a promise into reality."

The Role of Shared Values

Another basis on which building trust and commitment rests is in aligning values and priorities. If both partners share similar values-personal, financial, or moral-things get smoother. Shared values form the underlying framework that guides a relationship through difficult times.

Decisions become easier when values are aligned. Whether it is talking about finances, parenting styles, or life goals, shared values provide a common ground that reaffirms your commitment to each other. It fosters an environment where both partners feel respected and empowered to voice their opinions, resulting in deeper trust.

The Impact of Trust and Commitment

When you have trust and commitment in a relationship, it totally creates good vibes that go beyond just the two of you. Relationships built on these things usually have better emotional support, smoother communication, and just a higher emotional IQ between partners. You guys turn into teammates instead of opponents, tackling life's ups and downs side by side.

Plus, how a relationship is doing can really affect how people get along with others. When folks feel safe in their love, they go out into the world feeling way more confident, understanding, and nice. Trust and commitment create a vibe where the couple can really flourish, helping each other out while also making a good impact in the community.

In traditional communities, trust and commitment are the foundation for all social interactions and family bonds. They keep us grounded in our shared humanity, that we are all just imperfect folks looking to connect with each other. Relationships truly thrive when individuals work through trust because life's best moments usually lie in the journey of dealing with imperfections as a unit.

Conclusion: The Lifelong Journey

Building trust and commitment is a lifelong adventure, Don't you think? It's all about ongoing growth, learning, and bouncing back. You really have to be intentional, patient, and open to being vulnerable. Just like we grow and change as people, relationships do, too, and the trust and commitment between partners have to keep up with that.

So, starting this journey, just keep in mind that relationships are going to hit a few bumps here and there. When going gets tough, try to deal with it using kindness, a real sense of curiosity, and a teamwork vibe to get through it together. Create a space where you can be open and, share common values, and show your intentions through meaningful actions.

In the end, trust and commitment make love endure. They take those swift moments and make them memories you will carry with you, telling the story of strength, openness, and personal growth. By leaning into these concepts, you're not sharing space but building deep and meaningful connections. Throughout your journey of love, remember you both have differences, but together, you can form a solid foundation that will stand life's ups and downs—something that truly represents true and lasting love.

Key Takeaways

- Trust grows in small consistent moments .
- Stay committed at all levels emotionally, mentally and physically.
- Small gestures become the foundation for a resilient relationship.
- Conflicts and challenges are opportunities for growth and deeper understanding.
- Commitment is a choice: shown through consistent actions, support, and presence.
- Shared Values are a Guiding Compass.
- Trust and commitment strengthen relationships and creates positive emotional environments.

SECRET 16

TRANSFORMING CONFLICT INTO CONNECTION: HEALING THROUGH FORGIVENESS

"To forgive is the highest, most beautiful form of love. In return, you will receive untold peace and happiness."

– Robert Muller

Turning Conflict into Connection: Navigating Tough Times

So, love is usually seen as this perfect adventure—packed with happiness, giggles, and big dreams together. But the truth is, every real relationship has its fair share of fights and disagreements. I mean, you've got two totally different people with their own backgrounds, views, and feelings trying to mesh, and wherever there are people, differences are just a given. Rather than the destructive nature of conflict, it can be seen as a way through which people grow closer, understand each other, and become better. Even seemingly heated arguments can be seen as the way to strengthening relationships, if only because we are able to handle the powerful tool of forgiveness.

The Nature of Conflict in Relationships

Conflict is just part of love, right? It's like the best teacher we could ask for. It can totally unveil truths that we'd probably just ignore in our everyday hustle. Whether it's just a small spat over who does the dishes or some bigger stuff about our values and future goals, how we handle these conflicts can either push us apart or bring us closer together. I feel that this is an absolute truth. These conflicts show our true mettle to our partners.

Imagine a situation where your partner reacts harshly to a seemingly minor oversight. Instead of responding with frustration or annoyance, take a moment to consider what might be influencing their response. Perhaps they had a tough day at work, or they're dealing with underlying stress. By recognizing their struggles, you cultivate an emotional understanding that can diffuse tensions and facilitate compassion.

It can be good because it might bring sharp relief to those areas in the relationship that need attention and care. However, it is what we do with the conflict that determines whether we come out of it untouched or closer to one another.

Dealing with Conflict Curiously

One of the best ways to turn a fight into a bonding moment is by being curious. Instead of leaping to conclusions or guessing what your partner means, try to dive into the disagreement with real interest. Ask questions that help you both talk things out and get what each other is feeling instead of just getting defensive.

Think about this: you're in a heated argument about money. Instead of accusing your partner of being careless, ask him questions like, "Can you help me understand your perspective on our spending?" or "What do you feel when we talk about our budget?" These questions make your partner articulate his thoughts while showing him that you are ready to listen. When you make a space where you both can talk freely, you create a friendlier atmosphere to find common ground.

So, you know how Adam Grant, the author and organisational psychologist, says, **"Instead of judging others, we should try to think about what we can learn from them"?** Well, this idea totally applies to our relationships because our partners are basically our go-to teachers. When we keep a curious mindset during conflicts, it really helps us respect each other more and builds a stronger connection.

The Role of Empathy in Conflict Resolution

The next big tool for transformation from conflict into connection is empathy. If you can put yourself in your partner's shoes, you can understand and show more compassion. You may even be able to understand where they're coming from, even if you don't agree because you're seeing it through their eyes.

Suppose your partner has reacted to some small slip from you. Do not answer them in frustration or irritation; pause for a moment to ponder what might be the root cause of their response. Perhaps they have a rough day at work, or perhaps they have underlying tensions. Recognising those can help you gain emotional intelligence that can break down the tension and facilitate empathy.

You know, empathy is about more than just getting how someone feels; it also helps you communicate better. Instead of coming at them like it's an attack, you could say, "I can see you're really stressed right now. Let's talk about what's bothering you."

By doing this, you acknowledge your partner's feelings while also steering the conversation towards finding a solution and strengthening that connection.

Healing Power of Forgiveness

Perhaps the most crucial ingredient in turning conflict into connection is forgiveness. If the partner does not let go of a grievance, it then serves to create an emotional burden on him or her and ultimately will begin to poison the relationship. **But**

forgiveness is transformative- it sets both partners free and gives the relationship an opportunity to heal.

Forgiveness isn't just about brushing off the pain or acting like it never happened. Like Fred Luskin, a forgiveness researcher, says, **"Forgiveness is not about condoning the behaviour of others. It's about freeing yourself."** When you decide to forgive, you're really choosing to let go of all that anger or resentment that's been piling up from the fight.

Forgiveness is a process, not an event, and it takes time and work. Admit your feelings, and then find a healthy way to express them. Think about how your feelings affect you. This thought can move you away from the siren song of blame and toward understanding. Knowing that all people err—that you are included among the erring—cultivates acceptance that opens up the possibility of forgiveness.

Think of that old tale of star-crossed lovers in Shakespeare's "Romeo and Juliet". Their love story, full of drama from family fights, sadly ends in tragedy. But think, if the different characters had just gone for forgiveness, who knows? The love story could have turned out way differently—just a reminder that forgiveness can help resolve stuff instead of causing more drama.

Practical Steps to Cultivating Forgiveness

Creating a vibe of forgiveness in your relationship takes some effort. Here are some practical tips on how to make forgiveness a part of your healing process:

1. **Own Your Feelings**: Let those emotions flow. If you're feeling mad, sad, or just plain defeated, let yourself feel it. You can't start the path to forgiveness until you acknowledge what you're really feeling.
2. **Engage in Open Dialogue**: Share your feelings with your partner. Articulate your pain without assigning blame. Focus on using "I" statements to express how their actions impacted you.
3. **Shift Perspective**: Attempt to view the situation from your partner's perspective. This can help you understand their motivations and contribute to empathetic communication.
4. **Set Boundaries**: If a situation continues to create distress, be sure to communicate your boundaries. This can prevent similar conflicts in the future while promoting healthier interactions.
5. **Practise Generosity of Spirit**: Remind yourself that everyone is a work in progress. Just as you seek understanding from your partner, extend that same courtesy and have compassion for their imperfections.
6. **Forgive Yourself**: Very often, forgiveness of our own mistakes in a conflict is equally important. Own up to the role played, embrace growth, and stop the self-punishment.
7. **Make a Choice**: Forgiveness is always a choice. Remind yourself that the weight of holding resentment isn't bearable. Forgiveness becomes the choice for opening one's door to healing.

Building Bonds by Being Vulnerable

Building trust and commitment following conflict requires vulnerability. Sharing our true feelings—self-doubt, sadness, or fear—creates a connection that strengthens the bond between partners. It's this openness that reinforces trust, allowing both partners to feel safe in the relationship.

Being vulnerable helps us support one another. When one person is opening up, it normally makes the other want to open up. This back-and-forth really helps to strengthen our understanding and deepen our bond through those shared emotional moments.

Conclusion: Enjoying the Ride

Such an incredible journey that requires commitment, patience, and understanding to turn conflict into connection. Every relationship hits some bumps now and then; it's just part of being human. Instead of being scared of these tense moments, we can look at them as awesome chances to make our emotional ties even stronger.

By staying curious, showing empathy, and tapping into the healing vibes of forgiveness, we can turn challenges into wins. The love journey is all about the mix of fights and connections. These moments help us grow both as individuals and together, and in the end, we build a solid bond that can handle whatever life throws at us. And as Nelson Mandela said, **"Forgiveness liberates the soul. It removes fear."** That is why it is such a powerful weapon. When we practice forgiveness, we are letting go of the weight of anger and trauma, opening a door for healing that renews relationships.

As you go through the ups and downs of love, remember that a fight does not mean it is over; it is, in fact, a chance to grow. By being open and willing to forgive each other and tackle challenges as a team, you can really fortify your bond in trust and commitment. Love is such a journey, not a finish line, and the way to lasting love is filled with understanding, kindness, and the desire to turn conflict into connection again and again.

Conclusion of Part 4

In the process of travelling through the landscape of trust, conflict resolution, and healing, we find ourselves unveiling all the intricate dynamics that build our relationships. Trust becomes the bedrock of love while navigating conflicts with understanding and resilience allows us to come out stronger on the other side. And finally, when we embrace forgiveness, we create space for healing and renewal, transforming pain into an opportunity for a deeper connection.

So, you know, all these things really need a mix of grace and hard work. Don't stress about the imperfections; just tackle those challenges with an open heart. When we choose to trust, sort out conflicts well, and practice forgiveness, we make our relationships thrive and create this cosy space where love can blossom. Let these tips steer you as you keep moving along on this amazing journey of love!

PART 5

GROWTH AND TRANSFORMATION

Love isn't just something that stays constant; it's this amazing, living force that really shines when we grow and change. Think of it like a beautiful tree stretching up into the sky—real love needs care, flexibility, and being open to growing together. So, in this chapter, let's jump into the adventure of growing and evolving as partners—taking on changes, learning from each other, and cheering each other's dreams on.

SECRET 17

LOVE IS A JOURNEY, NOT A DESTINATION

"Let your joy be in your journey - not in some distant goal".

– Tim Cook

So, as I sit here writing down my thoughts on this profound topic, I can't help but feel a ton of emotions and gratitude. Love is such a beautiful word that covers so many meanings and feelings. It really is like a journey packed with fun twists, ups and downs, and a blend of happiness and sadness.

As we kick off this journey of love, it's so important to understand that love isn't just a place to get to, but more like a road we need to travel on. It's like a twisty path taking us to an unknown spot, and love comes with its own bumps and hurdles that we have to deal with smoothly and patiently.

The Sparkle of Love

Isn't it wonderful when you fall in love? It's like you've found the key to living your best life. Suddenly, everything around you seems way more vibrant, and it's all just buzzing with excitement, making every moment feel super meaningful. Being in love is like getting wrapped up in this cosy hug, kind of like walking into a sunny room packed with laughter; it's a vibe you'd want to stay in forever. You know those early days of romance? They're just full of colour, packed with adventure, fun chats, and so many new things to check out. But even in all that excitement, there might be this little voice popping up, asking you stuff like: Will this happiness stick around? Is this feeling just one awesome moment, ready to vanish like the colours of a sunset?

It is almost ironic how the fear of losing such great moments can make us miss them in reality. We hold onto love as if it were this fragile butterfly, thinking that if we squeeze it too tight, we will break it, but if we let go a little, it'll slip away. We forget that love isn't some finish line we are sprinting towards; it's more like this journey packed with beautiful moments that shape our relationships.

Love's journey is not an easy one. The ocean can get calm one minute and wild the next, and it is pretty much the same way. We have to prepare to ride out its rough patches and keep the faith and trust in each other strong. That is where our love really shines, lighting up shadows trying to pull us down.

Do you know, in those small everyday moments, we find out just what love is about—to share laughter over coffee, hug each other after an endless day, or maybe all the quiet, late-night whispers that simply lift you up? Other people may have such small moments in common, but for us, they form the base of our forever love.

Let's talk about what love really is. It's not the big things; it's not anniversaries, living together, or the classic white picket fence. Love is really part of our daily lives. There are moments of shared laughs over inside jokes, the comfortable feeling of holding hands while in a chill moment, and just having a companion who simply listens without saying anything else.

You know, these little moments add up and make this incredible feel of the experience that we have together. Even the smallest act adds to how we gain and share love. But when we are all worked up over what's next or if this will pass, we entirely miss the heart of our journey.

You know, in this crazy, fast-paced world we're living in, we rush through our relationships. We are so focused on trying to figure out what's going to happen in the future, like, what is our life going to be like in five years? We totally miss the amazing stuff that's happening right now. Love really blooms in the moment, in the present, and it's such a privilege to feel it, no matter how long it sticks around.

Accepting Uncertainty

I mean, life can be so unpredictable, and love is just not an exception. When you fall for someone that hard, it can be incredible, but the vulnerability just kind of feels like a double-edged sword. And when we open ourselves to love, we also put ourselves at risk for hurt. Relationships can crumble; they can just wither away or change into something else. But aren't all those risks, though, just totally worth it for love?

Remember how beautiful a sunset can be? It is just amazing and deep but doesn't last long. We don't ignore sunsets because they are short-lived; we rather enjoy every single one for its unique colours and the way it transforms everything. Love's also kind of the same way, right? Sure, some of those moments might not come back, but if we're always preparing for loss, we miss out on really enjoying the happiness of the moment.

We should just chill and be in the moment, really tune into our feelings, and soak up love in all its different shapes. Instead of stressing over whether the happiness we're feeling will stick around forever, uncertainty is what makes love so exciting, makes the good times feel even better, and makes the bond stronger.

The Lasting Mark of Love

You know, even relationships that don't last can really leave a mark on us. Every connection, no matter how long it lasts, teaches us something important. It can change how we see ourselves and the people around us, helping us grow in ways we didn't expect. When we let love guide our journey, we end up richer and more knowledgeable—including how we deal with future partners.

A short-lived love really teaches us to cherish life in all its highs and lows, proving how great it is to live every moment to the fullest. Of course, it is easy to get carried away with long-term relationships, but the goodness of love matters far more than how long it lasts.

When we decide to open our hearts to love, it only becomes a question of giving the best for ourselves. Every little moment-like snuggling up for a movie on a lazy Sunday, cooking dinner together after a hectic day, or just dreaming out loud about what we want- makes this journey so rich. It is only through opening up our hearts to love and letting every experience happen naturally that we are freed of all those pesky expectations that help create a deeper connection.

The Joy of the Journey

Love isn't about where you are going but about the journey you take. Every smile shared, every tear cried, and every challenge faced together matters. Instead of stressing over whether your relationship will hit some ideal endpoint, think about what joy means in the whole picture of your love. Let joy be your guide as you figure out the ups and downs of relationships; try to build not just a legacy of love but a path filled with gratitude and appreciation.

Remember to enjoy every moment of this magnificent journey of love. Enjoy the little things, be good, and build beautiful memories that are deeply etched in your heart. Appreciate every minute, and do not watch the clock or worry about the future. This moment is what counts.

Conclusion: An Invitation to Enjoy

Love is all about appreciating the journey, you know? In a world that usually focuses on getting to the finish line and what we achieve, it's like a reminder to just enjoy the ride with all its highs and lows and those every day and amazing moments. Seriously, love isn't just some goal we're trying to hit; it's all those countless moments that mould us into who we are and who we'll be.

So go ahead, open your heart, and fully embrace love! Savour the laughter and the challenges, the quiet moments and the delightful chaos, the fleeting instances and the everlasting connections. It's the beautiful journey of love—full of its wonderful complexities that truly enriches life. Let's dive into every moment, embracing everything as it comes, and allowing love to blossom in all its unpredictability. After all, the greatest gift is not in what we possess, but in the heartfelt journey we share with one another.

Hope we all get the courage to jump into this love adventure, even if where we're headed is a mystery, as this journey is full of beauty, joy, and endless possibilities. Love isn't somewhere to arrive; it's a journey that's supposed to be enjoyed with hearts wide open. And while on this journey, let's discover the secret of eternal love.

SECRET 18

TIME AND SPACE IN LOVE: THE MAGIC INGREDIENTS

"Love is the one thing we're capable of perceiving that transcends dimensions of time and space. Maybe we should trust that, even if we can't understand it."

– Dr. Brand

So, when it comes to love, we have to juggle time and space, right? They're these powerful things that really shape our relationships. It's like how a skilled chef blends different ingredients to whip up something amazing; love grows through the awesome mix of time and space. If we just embrace and get these unique bits, we unlock the secrets to building strong connections.

The Timeless Journey of Love

At first glance, love might seem like it blossoms overnight. A spark could ignite within a second that sends butterflies fluttering in our stomachs and fills our hearts with excitement. However, the truth is that true love does not appear overnight in an explosion; rather, it gradually unfolds as time passes and shared experiences and mutual understanding are intertwined.

Think of time as the quiet architect of love, creating a deepening connection. It is in those quiet moments spent together, filled with laughter, tears, vulnerability, and growth, that love truly takes root. This journey is all about taking our time. The more love and care we pour into our partnerships, the more vibrant and meaningful our connections become.

In our fast-paced world, we always forget the beautiful value of patience. With everything on our fingertips, it's easy to wish our relationships could mirror the speed of our digital lives. Yet, true love blooms steadily, encouraging us to embrace our feelings, letting them grow naturally, and nurturing them through cherished moments together. When love stands the test of time, it transforms into a deep, lasting bond—an eternal love that gracefully withstands life's challenges.

Time as a Teacher and Healer

Time not only nurtures us with care; it's like an awesome teacher and healer too. In every relationship, there are times when things get rocky. Whether it's misunderstandings, bad vibes, or those curveballs life throws at us, these things can really create gaps. But hey, the cool thing is that time lets us sort through our stuff and helps us understand our feelings way better. It reminds us of being flexible and willing to sacrifice for the sake of another person, because love is not a destination but a journey.

Think about this: whenever there is a problem in a relationship, it's really easy to get overwhelmed by frustration and sadness.

When things get tough, it's easy to forget that time has a special knack of softening the rough edges of pain. With a little patience, we can be clear in our minds, heal the wounds, and rediscover a deep appreciation for our partners. Taking just that moment to breathe, reflect, and let ourselves grow can really mend our relationships and strengthen our bonds.

The Delicate Balance of Space

Space, the other half of our equation, plays a beautiful role in our relationship with time.

When you're in love, making a shared space just for you two is super important! When partners let each other into their personal worlds, they create this unique little universe together—a comfy spot where being open and vulnerable really works. Balancing that special space with the need for personal time feels kind of like walking a tightrope. It needs a nice mix of being independent and being together. Being independent lets us chase our own passions and interests, while being together gives us that awesome feeling of belonging and connection. Each partner needs the chance to grow, learn, and find out who they really are; funny enough, this personal space actually makes the bond even stronger. Love really thrives when neither partner feels suffocated or ignored. It grows best when both people can just be themselves and also have each other's backs completely.

The Challenge of Long-Distance Love

When talking about space, we cannot forget the complications of long-distance relationships. In our globalized world, people are bound to find love across geographical lines. However, despite all the advances in communication technology, the distance can create a palpable tension and sense of longing. The absence can be overwhelming, and the challenge of maintaining a connection over time requires extraordinary commitment and maturity.

Long distance relationships truly make love put to the test, challenging partners to actually make an effort in bridging the gap. In a situation where one is not able to experience togetherness, warm hugs, and exciting celebrations, one can feel emotionally burdened. But then, this is not all; on the contrary, it provokes couples to come up with more creative ways to stay connected virtually by regular video calls, sweet messages and even doing things together online.

You know that saying, "Absence makes the heart grow fonder"? Well, these challenges really remind me of it. When we're not together, it usually makes us miss each other and appreciate one another a whole lot more.

Embracing Journey of Time and space

Having some time apart is a great chance to think about how we feel, remember how committed we are, and really understand just how much our partners mean to us.

The key, then, lies in how we choose to see it; distance is at the same time both a barrier and a bridge toward the strengthening of the connection relationship. Embracing the Journey of Time and Space As we explore the beautiful complexities of love, let's cherish the journey that time and space provide.

Love isn't just about where we end up; it's about the wonderful experiences we share, the important lessons we learn, and the personal growth we achieve along the way. Time helps us cultivate patience, healing, and deeper understanding, while space encourages a sense of independence, trust, and appreciation.

So, like, it's crucial to keep in mind that every moment we spend building our love—whether we're hanging out or doing our own thing—really adds to what we're putting into it with our hearts. Those strong connections we build over time, instead of just some passing feelings, are what really lay the groundwork for relationships that last. When both people get how crucial time and space are, they create this awesome mix that totally boosts their love, making it lively and exciting.

Conclusion: The Magic Ingredients of Love

So, basically, time and space are essential for love. They really shape our connections, making it clear that love grows not just in those fun times we share, but also when we have our own space. The whole love thing takes a lot of patience, thinking things through, and being flexible, and having some space—whether it's physical or emotional—helps us build trust and really appreciate each other.

If we go with the flow of time and space, we could actually create a vibe where love really grows. All relationships are unique because the people in it have had their own different experiences and backgrounds. Seeing time and space as very important in our love lives makes connections that are both meaningful and long-lasting.

SECRET 19

EMBRACING CHANGE AND GROWTH: SHARED VISIONS AND CELEBRATING LIFE'S JOURNEY

"The secret of change is to focus all of your energy not on fighting the old, but on building the new"

– Socrates

Getting Old Together is a really beautiful thing in this beautiful journey of Love,. It is not about how many years we pile on; it is really all about the strong connection we build while experiencing everything life throws at us. The core of a long-lasting relationship is all about how we handle change, root for each other's growth, and happily celebrate our shared dreams for the future together.

The Beauty of Evolving Together

Look at the beginning of any love story, right? We usually get totally caught up in that first spark-the whole magic of romance that just knocks us off our feet and makes us feel on cloud nine. But those awesome moments of happiness are really just the beginning of a relationship that needs some care and flexibility. Love isn't just something that sits still; it's this ever-changing thing that needs our focus, dedication, and most importantly, the openness to grow.

You know, as we go through life, relationships have to change with both the world around us and within us. This means stuff like new jobs, family situations, health issues, and personal growth all influence who we become, both as people and as partners. So, love isn't simply keeping things the same but really is about growing together, finding strength in what makes us different, and turning challenges into chances to connect.

So, love's journey is kind of like a rollercoaster, right? There are ups and downs; happy times and sad; wins and losses. It lets you see each other's good and bad sides—that's what true love gets you through the tough times and hangs onto hope for better days ahead. Dealing with all these highs and lows takes not just sticking it out but also serious grit.

Consider the moments that test our relationships: loss of jobs, health scares, or loss of loved ones. These experiences can shake the very foundation of a partnership, yet they also provide vital opportunities for growth. Just as nature endures seasonal changes, so does a healthy relationship through adversity. The ability to communicate openly during difficult times creates a sense of safety and security, reinforcing the foundations of the partnership.

Such couples are the ones that truly create a space to be supportive and motivating enough to each other. This simply means that one partner can be totally motivating for the other, even lighting a spark within them that activates personal growth. It is within the raw moments of sharing fears and victories that love gets even stronger.

Falling in Love Again and Again

It is actually fascinating when you fall in love. Many relationships lead to a cosy routine where that initial excitement tends to wear off. However, that spark can definitely be brought back by making an effort to appreciate each other amidst all the craziness life throws at you.

Great relationships thrive not just on those big romantic gestures but also on those small, everyday things we do for each other that really make our connections stronger. You know, a genuine "I believe in you" on a rough day or a supportive "You've got this" can totally change a regular moment into something special that shows we care. It's crucial to celebrate the little wins—whether it's getting a new promotion, hitting a personal goal, or just making it through a tough time—to really enjoy our journey together in life.

This creates a vibe where the partners can chase their dreams but still keep the relationship strong. The aim is to create a love that grows through the experiences you share, grounded in respect and appreciation for each other.

Making a Joint Vision

Thinking about the future together is really a big part of the journey as love grows. What do you imagine for yourselves in five, ten, or twenty years? Having a shared vision helps both partners align their personal dreams so as to make way for a life that thrills and inspires them both.

Thinking about the future, whether it is stuff like money issues, expanding the family, or travel goals or even the more touchy-feely things like emotional support and making memories together, really helps map out where you're headed. Talking regularly about your dreams and what you expect keeps the relationship lively and fresh, letting both of you adjust as your ideas change. Plus, it can help make sense of what each other cares about so that you guys can work together toward something bigger.

Basically, the shared vision isn't only about where you want to end up. It's about the values and dreams that bring everyone together. Cheering each other on and helping with each other's goals is what really makes a strong partnership last. When both partners put their energy into building a life they're stoked about; the payoffs just get bigger.

Celebrate the Journey of Life

Well, you know, celebration is all about love. It's just about recognising those special moments and milestones that pop up. When we celebrate life's journey together, it really strengthens our bond. Whether we are marking anniversaries, personal wins, or just enjoying the little everyday things, noticing these moments brings a wave of gratitude and appreciation.

These marks may be small celebrations, special dinners to share after a long week, spontaneous weekend trips, or even rituals around movie nights. Acknowledging ups and downs, as well as turning points into growth, fosters an attitude of gratitude that enriches love.

Moreover, celebration is a reminder to reflect on the journey thus far: the memories created, the challenges faced, and the love that has deepened over time. It elevates the ordinary into something extraordinary, aligning partners in a collective sense of purpose and joy.

The Inevitability of Change

Change, with all its ups and downs, is just a part of life. Couples need to think of change as something crucial and a stepping stone for growth. It really drives home how important it is to be adaptable in a world where nothing stays the same.

When partners recognise that change is not something to fear but rather an opportunity for transformation, they unlock infinite potential in their relationship. Whether it's changes in careers, family structures, or life circumstances, embracing the ebb and flow fosters creativity and resilience. Couples who understand and accept this dynamic are often better equipped to navigate the ups and downs of life.

Conclusion: The Journey Awaits

You know, when it comes to love, openness to change and growth is helps in getting closer to each other. As you and your partner grow together, you build a strong and adaptable relationship that can handle life's ups and downs. You guys have a shared vision that pushes you both towards new adventures, enjoying all the crazy stuff life throws your way while keeping that connection alive with support, forgiveness, and happiness.

Love's a journey, right? It's this twisty road packed with ups and downs but also these beautiful moments that we need to hold on to. The key to forever love isn't just about cosy companionship; it's also about having the guts to change, grow, and dive into those shared adventures coming our way. When couples understand that every moment, every little change, and every celebration adds to the richness of love, then they can create a life journey that's lively, fulfilling and lasts forever.

While they hang out and live these moments, they totally become each other's biggest friends. Growing in a relationship is not about getting through life's tough stuff; it's all about thriving together, cheering on each other's passions, and picking up lessons from whatever life throws their way. It's this awesome dance of change that weaves their dreams together, shaping them into not just solo artists but partners in creativity.

Growth can feel daunting, especially when faced with significant life changes. However, as Ralph Waldo Emerson wisely said, **"The only person you are destined to become is the person you decide to be."** In love, we must embrace the reality of evolving together. Celebrate those moments—big or small—when you support each other's journeys. Learn together. Failure and success alike become shared memories that deepen your bond.

True love is not about being in a comfortable routine; it really shines when things get a little challenging. When we stop being scared of what we don't know and aim to grow together, we build a relationship that can handle any tough times and celebrate every happy moment.

Conclusion Part 5

As we close up this journey into growth and transformation, we see how shared experiences, helping each other out, and celebrating together are very important in nurturing love. So, embrace the changes, back each other's dreams, and make those shared visions; that's how we evolve together!

Love is a journey within itself, full of adventure, learning about oneself and about each other. When we really follow this journey, dedicating ourselves to growth, identifying our goals, and marking down memories we made, then it's what builds a relationship rich with depth and life.

Alright, let's move forward with open hearts and really commit to fostering that amazing transformation love can bring. Let's cherish the journey, care for one another, and step into a path that will take us to deeper intimacy and connection. Together, we should make sure that our love stories are not about getting through difficult times but are lively adventures packed with joy, laughter, and endless growth!

PART 6

MOVING ON

Moving on from a relationship can feel akin to standing at the precipice of a cliff, where a fierce wind lashes against you, rendering each step fraught with uncertainty. Yet, it is also a moment of profound empowerment, an opportunity to reclaim your life and rediscover your happiness. This chapter encompasses moving on and some relevant red flag behaviours within relations, teaching the art of healing with a broken heart, and getting needed support through counselling when the occasion calls for that. Moving forward is ours together now.

SECRET 20

RECOGNISING AND RESPONDING TO TOXICITY: IDENTIFYING RED FLAGS

"The red flags you ignore in the beginning will be the reason why you'll be unhappy in the relationship; They will also be the reason it eventually ends."

– Jillian Turacki

When we enter into a relationship, we do so with hopeful hearts, dreams, and that thrilling feeling of love. At its core, love is much more than just romantic attraction; it is a deep concern for each other, offering each other support in the hardest of times and the deepest respect for one's emotional well-being. It means you love your partner as an individual with thoughts, feelings, and ambitions. But as we venture through the intricacies of love, we sometimes struggle with subtle signs of toxicity that even perfect relationships might allow to seep into their system. If we are to hold on to love and respect as a means to keep our relationships going, we need to know when these red flags emerge early enough. So, let us look deeper.

Love is not just about attraction.

First and foremost, it's imperative to remember what two people unite for. The most significant reason is love. And love is definitely more than those short-term butterflies when one is smitten with someone. It entails creating an environment where partners can be themselves, uplifting each other and dignifying their individuality as well. When we honestly love, we create that atmosphere conducive to growth and understanding while respecting each other.

But what happens when this foundation starts to crack? How does it manifest itself when love turns into restlessness, discontent, or even toxicity? It is very often a subtle transition and might leave one or both partners unaware of it until it becomes something quite substantial.

The Warning Signs of Toxicity

If you feel unease within your relationship, it then becomes crucial to look for clear signs of toxicity. Just like most relationships have their fair share of ups and downs, there are certain behaviours that indicate a bigger issue at play. Some of the following red flags to watch out for:

1. **Constant Unpleasantness**: Should your interactions be laden with negativity—filled with arguments, criticism, or disrespect—you might be ensnared in toxicity. A loving relationship ought to bring joy and comfort, not a steady stream of conflict and strife.
2. **Feeling Suffocated**: Healthy relationships permit personal space. If you sense that your individuality is being eclipsed or you are consistently overwhelmed by your partner's demands, it may indicate a toxic dynamic.
3. **Neglect and Undermining**: A lover who consistently denies your sentiments or ambitions can seriously reduce your emotional health. Anyone deserves to be listened to and valued; without that essential support, resentment can set in.
4. **Unbalanced Effort**: A relationship should be a give-and-take; there should be effort from both sides to contribute and reap. When one person continuously gives and the other continuously takes, this can develop an unhealthy power dynamic.
5. **Fear and Intimidation**: No one in a loving relationship should ever feel frightened or intimidated. If the actions or words of your partner leave you feeling nervous, you should confront the fear head-on.

Red flags in relationships frequently whisper their warnings before they escalate into shouts, urging us to remain vigilant. It is essential to keep in mind that love should always enhance your sense of self-worth. Indicators such as verbal aggression, efforts to control your behaviour, or attempts to isolate you from friends may signify toxic dynamics. As Maya Angelou wisely stated, **"When someone shows you who they are, believe them the first time."**

This way, you can be protected from the red flags in a relationship that is not going to make you happy. Surrounding yourself with supportive friends and family proves invaluable, as they can provide insightful perspectives. Keep your ears open to their concerns; love has a way of obscuring our judgment, making it all too simple to miss the reality unfolding around us.

Respect is Important

Respect forms the base of any healthy relationship. It fundamentally speaks of the other's dignity and worth as a human being. It follows that if respect is slipping away through misunderstandings or, bad communication or complacency, things begin to break down. People sometimes disagree, not wanting to hear another view. In fairness, it's a two-way journey because love does not only grow but lives off mutual respect.

That is when the relationship begins to fall when you stop listening to one another and start becoming the most important person in every situation. The base of a relationship is cooperation; instead of letting the differences split the couple, they celebrate and work together.

Managing Conflicts

Every couple fights; it is a natural part of any relationship. However, the key to a healthy partnership lies in how these disagreements are managed. Constant fighting can lead to emotional exhaustion, breeding a sense of hopelessness that can permeate the relationship.

This is where effective communication comes in. Conflicts need to be resolved promptly and effectively. Do not drag your arguments on for days, festering into resentments. Communicate and find solutions that make the two parties valued and understood. Good communication is the backbone of positive relationships, wherein one does not fear retaliation.

Toxic Cycle

Why does anyone stick around in a toxic relationship? That is what most might ask themselves in relation to their situation. Painfully, love has the effect of blinding the obvious. Perhaps one is afraid of loneliness; perhaps one hopes things will improve. Perhaps, between all this toxicity, there remain shards of love that bound you together.

Another practical reason why many women continue to endure toxic relationships is their financial dependence on men, which leaves them fearful of being left without a home.

Recent studies indicate that many individuals find it challenging to exit toxic relationships because they cling to old memories and feelings. However, it's crucial to understand that love is important but not the sole reason to sustain a relationship.

Reflection and Introspection

If you're experiencing any of the toxicity signs mentioned earlier, it's time for serious introspection. Reflect on your relationship and ask yourself:

Does anxiety or fear of my partner commonly occur? Do I feel loved and appreciated by my partner? Are my emotional needs met in this relationship?

Your emotional well-being is always to come first. If one is in a deeply loving relationship, nobody should ever want to harm another, and no one's other half should ever have their dignity diminished or their well-being threatened. These introspective thoughts may just leave you knowing that your relationship does indeed harm more than it loves you.

Creating a Thought-Out Plan

In case you resolve to challenge toxic tendencies, planning will be your best approach. You begin by having an open conversation with your partner. State your concerns directly and candidly, yet be prepared to listen at the same time. Some partners are completely unaware of the effects their actions produce and may open up for change once made aware.

If the thought of confrontation scares you, prepare yourself mentally for this discussion. You know your partner best—consider his or her temperament and how he or she might react. Try to have a calm, private setting so that both of you may speak freely without external pressures.

When to Seek Help

If you feel that the conversation is becoming too heavy to bear alone, or if it starts becoming unhealthy in nature, such as emotional or physical abuse, then it might be a good idea to get additional support. Professional therapists can provide a safe environment and excellent communication strategies, which in turn allows both partners to traverse their conflicts more easily. They can also assist individuals in processing their feelings and identifying behaviour patterns that might be holding them back from health.

Moving Forward

No one ever enters into a relationship thinking that it is going to become toxic, but life has ways of surprising us that we cannot even imagine. Therefore, it is necessary to stay alert and attentive to both yourself and your partner. The signs of toxicity will save you from emotional turmoil and lead you toward a healthier, more fulfilling love life.

Remember that the relationship should create happiness, nurturing, and growth as a healthy and loving relationship. It should be about two people growing with each other while pushing the other to be better; they should enjoy every moment—accepting the ups and downs of life ahead.

As you begin this journey, strive to build a relationship founded upon respect, with open communication and understanding. Such a pursuit is beautiful, though it may demand effort and commitment, yet it remains something undeniably worth the undertaking. Love is meant to be uplifting and inspiring, so it's not something to avoid when searching for the joy that a healthy relationship can bring about. After all, it should feel like home, not a battleground.

SECRET 21

A NEW DAWN: EMBRACING THE ART OF MOVING ON

"Accept yourself, love yourself, and keep moving forward. If you want to fly, you have to give up what weighs you down."

– Roy T. Bennett

Emotional Pain of a Heartbreak

In the rollercoaster ride of love, we are liable to soar to dizzying heights and plunge into depths that leave us breathless. It feels like a part of us is broken irreparably when a relationship ends. After investing all we have—our emotions, our time, our trust, and our faithful devotion—the crumbling of it all at once can feel like betrayal not only by our partner but by the universe itself. It feels as though the cosmos has conspired to topple our dreams and plunge us into an abyss of yearning and loss.

In these moments of profound sorrow, everything appears warped. The shadows of bygone memories linger like spectres at every turn. No matter how we try to distract ourselves, our minds always seem to reverberate with the sweet melodies of laughter we shared, the quiet moments we spent together, and the dreams once twinkling like stars dispersed in the night sky.

We question ourselves with this unrelenting fervour: What could I have done differently? Why did I not notice the signs? The emotional ache may be all-consuming, draped in the bittersweet sting of music that resonates with our pain.

Heartbreak can resemble a tidal wave crashing down—overwhelming, unpredictable, and relentless. Yet, it's essential to remember that moving on does not imply shutting love out.

As the poet Rumi beautifully expressed, **"The wound is the place where the Light enters you."** Each heartbreak imparts vital lessons about ourselves, our desires, and the significance of what we cherish. It's a journey toward rediscovering your passions, strengths, and what you genuinely seek in a relationship.

The Depth of Loss

It is important to grasp the magnitude of heartbreak. It is more than a romantic disappointment; it is a deep emotional disquiet. The loss of someone close—whether by separation or change in emotion—sets up a web of regrets and persistent 'what-ifs.' One feels caught in the eye of a storm, where the winds of doubt and grief blow unremittingly. Your professional life may deteriorate as you start to enter deep introspection, while at the same time weakening all ties with family.

In these challenging moments, it is essential to hold onto a simple yet profound mantra: **"God, grant me the serenity to accept the things I cannot change, the courage to change the things I can, and the wisdom to know the difference."** This wisdom marks the beginning of our journey toward healing. It involves learning to distinguish between what is salvageable and what has become nothing more than a memory.

Evaluating the Circumstances

Before proceeding, which would most likely be an emotional drive and determination, one needs to come to a standstill and ponder the situation for a bit. One must ask those difficult questions: is the relationship salvageable? Are the feelings returning? Can there be hope to rekindle the love they once had? Should one determine that the bond is worth saving- if the love still glimmers somewhere beneath the embers- then muster up enough courage and give it your all.

However, if the answer is no, if you start to realise that the person you loved has indeed left or that rekindling that love is impossible, then it is time to face the reality of your loss. Heartbreak can, at times, weave into our emotions such anguish that it can frequently obscure our viewpoint, obscuring the distinction between hope and delusion. At times, the most courageous expression of love is letting go.

Letting Go: The Way to Move On

Moving on is not an easy task, nor is it something that happens overnight. It's a journey that requires patience, bravery, and, most of all, deep self-reflection. When we hang onto what has outlived its purpose, we let the fear of what's yet to come guide our choices. The fear of solitude, the fear of transformation, and the fear of never loving again bind us to what's been and prevent us from embracing new possibilities that lie ahead of us.

Understand that you are not alone in this journey. Countless others face the same challenges. Accepting the act of letting go can be one of the most liberating experiences, acting as a necessary step to healing. Though your heart feels heavy, with time, every small act of self-care will gradually lighten your emotional load.

Let me share my own story with you. About 25 years ago, I was in the lively city of Pune. busy in a training course to shape my career in the army. It was during this period that love unexpectedly entered into my life like a cool breeze. I was young and bubbling with energy, busy in the rigours of military training, when I met her through a common friend— a girl who opened my eyes to a new meaning of connection and affection.

From the moment we met, it felt as if sparks flew between us, igniting quite an intensity. It was love at first sight. She was indeed pretty, and we clicked instantly, sharing laughter, dreams, and moments that felt like straight from the fabric of a fairytale. Our dates were mostly joyful bike rides through Pune, and every stolen moment together felt precious.

Yet, the reality of our situation was hard to ignore. My time in Pune was brief, and I needed to head back to my posting in Jammu and Kashmir. What had started as an exciting romance soon faced the challenge of distance? Over the next three years, we poured our hearts into keeping our love alive, sending letters of hope, dreams and missing each other, long-distance phone calls (It was a big challenge to make phone calls in those days), and of course, not to forget, my visits back and forth to the city where we had created so many fond treasured memories together.

We dreamed of our future together, talking about marriage and the family we envisioned. Our hearts felt immense joy with hopes and aspirations, and we truly believed that love could bridge any distance, any gap.

However, as days turned into months, the strain of being separated began to cast shadows over our once-vibrant connection. Gradually, the cracks widened, and despite our sincere efforts, the burden of separation became a challenge too great to bear. Ultimately, after about three years of a wonderful relationship, we made the fateful decision to part ways—a sorrow that created a deep wound within my soul.

In the wake of our split, I endured an emotional upheaval. I was deeply distressed, feeling lost and hopeless. The dreams we had spun together had crashed like fragile glass, shattered in an instant. I struggled to find focus in my job, my studies, and even the hobbies that once filled me with joy. The heaviness of lost love was a lot to carry, making it hard to see that any hope for brighter days could be on the horizon. In those moments of deep sadness, it felt like my journey in love had come to a painful end.

Just when it seemed like there was no way forward, slowly, a wonderful realisation came slowly to light. I started to understand that this tough chapter wasn't the end of my story but rather a closed door leading to new opportunities.

What I had gone through became a beautiful lesson in love, loss, and resilience, building strength within me that I was just beginning to discover. I felt as if the universe, in its infinite wisdom, was gently guiding me toward a fresh start.

This beautiful period of reflection truly opened my heart to new horizons. I realised that love, in its many wonderful forms, could unexpectedly find its way back into my life.

Everything changed for me when Ritu stepped in; her presence was like a refreshing breeze and a bright new light. At that time, I was stationed in Punjab, and the army was on high alert during Operation Parakram. Yet, love has a way of surprising you! Ritu was not only beautiful but also incredibly smart—a girl who carried herself with such confidence, though she seemed just a bit out of reach.

Our relationship blossomed slowly; even though we were both a little hesitant at first, we gradually opened up to each other. I felt at ease sharing my past with her, and she was nothing short of understanding and caring, accepting me wholeheartedly.

Then began our beautiful days of courtship, and I created many delightful memories with her—romantic outings, bike rides to scenic locations, stolen moments of togetherness away from prying eyes, and even lovely visits to spiritual places to deepen our love for each other.

Throughout the past 21 years of our marriage, every single day has been a memorable journey filled with love and joy, offering us new perspectives on the magic of love. It's been truly wonderful to soak in the beautiful treasures of moments that have brought us together.

As I stepped into this new chapter of life alongside Ritu, I joyfully embraced the incredible opportunity for love that God had gifted me. I found a renewed sense of resilience and openness, treasuring every lesson from my past as we created beautiful new memories together. Over the years, we have evolved through a number of shared experiences that have shaped our beautiful love to this day.

I've come to realise that love has never let me down; it's always been a wondrous journey of exploration—one that continues to unfold more beautifully with each new day.

Evaluating the Circumstances

Before moving forward, often fuelled by emotional drive and determination, it is essential to pause for a moment and reflect on the situation. One must grapple with those challenging questions: Is the relationship salvageable? Are the feelings returning? Is there hope to reignite the love that once flourished? Should one feel that the bond is worth saving- if the love still glimmers somewhere beneath the embers- then muster up enough courage and give it your all?

But if the answer is no—if you start to realise that the person you once loved has really gone or that rekindling that love is impossible—then it is time to face the truth of your loss. Heartbreak can weave such pain into our emotions that it often obscures our view, blurring the line between hope and delusion. Sometimes, the bravest act of love is simply letting go.

Letting Go: The Path to Moving On

To move on is no easy pursuit or overnight event. It requires patience, courage, and, above all, the hardest form of self-reflection. When we hold on to something that has long fulfilled its purpose, we become controlled by the fear of what may come next. The fear of loneliness, the fear of change, and the fear of never having love again tie us down to our past, and we cannot let go of the possibility that may await us in the future.

Understand that you are not alone on this journey; thousands of others share the same challenges. Letting go can become one of the most liberating experiences, which is a very important step toward healing. Though your heart feels heavy now, with time, each small act of self-care will slowly lighten your emotional burden.

Looking for Support and Guidance

Let's look into a very liberating concept: the idea of asking for help. There is no shame in seeking support or help from friends, family, or professionals. In fact, it is a bold step toward healing and personal growth. It can be likened to a compass that guides one back from a foggy sea towards the peaceful shores you hope to find.

Seeking guidance from loved ones or professionals can provide priceless perspectives and tools to help navigate the path of healing. Whether it's therapy, support groups, or just confiding in a trusted friend, these connections can illuminate your way forward.

A New Dawn: Your Life Awaits

As you slowly emerge from the mist of heartbreak and begin embracing this beautiful journey of moving on, remember that one chapter closing doesn't necessarily mean that your story has ended. It presents a tremendous opportunity for reinvention. Imagine your life as a canvas, and it is yours to fill it with a vivid depiction of your dreams.

As you think back on that relationship, consider the lessons you learned, the beautiful times you had, and all the love that grew out of that. That path has helped shape the great person you have become today, but that does not need to define the future. Rather, take it as a stepping stone to finding your own strength and the incredible ability you hold to love.

The great open plains of a brand-new day await you, full of potential, love, and so many possibilities. Move onward with an open heart because surely the universe, in its infinite wisdom, must hold the most fabulous plan imaginable for you, filled with experiences more fantastic than you would have ever conjured in your mind. Take another step; you have everything within yourself to move into a new stage of life. So, never forget to enjoy all those moments as you march on.

Moving forward doesn't mean forgetting the past; it is welcoming the future. So, as you move on, do not forget to leave your heart open for love waiting there for you. You are capable of converting your pain into personal growth, and by doing that, you guarantee that you will come out of this situation wiser and even stronger.

The path of improvement may call you to reassess what you truly need, but this is only the beginning. It is important to remember that you deserve love that lifts you up and inspires you, so never settle for less than that. Give yourself the grace to move forward with your heart open once again to the magical possibilities of love.

Conclusion of Part 6

We have been through all the crucial steps of moving on in this chapter, from recognising red flags to learning how to mend after heartbreak and why seeking help is important. Love is such a strong force, but it should never compromise your well-being or self-worth.

As you keep these understandings close to your heart, moving forward is sure to usher in deep and meaningful personal transformation. Trust yourself: you are strong enough to learn from the past, embracing hope and optimism about the future. Let your heart heal; allow it to embrace the limitless love that waits ahead.

Together, let's honour the journeys we've taken and the lessons we've learned. Love may occasionally lead us through challenging paths, but it will always guide us back to ourselves, stronger and ready to embrace new horizons. Let your heart be a beacon of hope, lighting the way for love to return anew!

Conclusion: The Infinite Power of Love

As we draw this journey through the vast realm of love to a close, it becomes vital to ponder the significant lessons we have uncovered together. Love, at its core, stands as the most formidable force within our grasp. It moulds our lives, affects our happiness, and shapes our experiences. From the roots of self-love to the intricate interplay of relationships, each chapter has illuminated a crucial facet that encourages us to embrace our greatest potential.

We started with the realisation that "self-love" is not an act of selfishness; rather, it serves as the foundation of every healthy relationship. By cherishing ourselves, we nurture the confidence necessary to forge and sustain bonds with others. Recognising our worth gives rise to a love that emanates outward, enhancing the lives of all those around us. As the Bhagavad Gita says, **"One who is not disturbed by the dualities of happiness and distress. is certainly eligible for liberation."** This is a very deep-rooted principle that reminds me self-acceptance is the basis of love.

The journey through familial love unravelled the beautiful cycle connecting generations. Through embracing love from our families and giving it to the next generation, we create legacies that last for generations. The cycle calls us to ponder our origins while building relationships based on gratitude, respect, and shared values.

Balancing emotional intimacy, vulnerability, and communication led us to understand that love is akin to a delicate dance that demands both grace and practice. Embracing the joys of togetherness while acknowledging the importance of boundaries permits love to thrive without sacrificing individuality.

Our exploration of conflict resolution and overcoming toxic relationships reinforced the notion that challenges are not signs of failure but rather opportunities for growth. Every obstacle can become a stepping stone, and every heartbreak is a chance to learn. In the words of J.K. Rowling, **"Failures are fuel for your growth."** Embracing this mindset empowers us to see love as a commitment to continual growth and improvement.

As the Bhagavad Gita wisely notes, **"You have the right to perform your prescribed duties, but you are not entitled to the fruits of your actions."** This urges us to concentrate on the art of nurturing love, free from the burdens of attachment to outcomes, reminding us to treasure the journey instead of fixating on swift results.

Let's recognise the paradox of love when we celebrate it, as it can bring immeasurable joy yet also usher in intense pain. With this double-edged sword, one understands how to nurture resilience and depth in relationships. And the more complex the love is, the more magnificent it is.

As you close this book, take time to reflect upon several principles to carry with you on where your journey with love might take you.

1. **Practice self-love**: Start your day each morning with the affirmation that will strengthen the sense of worth within yourself. Keep yourself immersed in activities that nurture your spirit, and make sure to celebrate your distinctive qualities.
2. **Develop Empathy**: Put a little effort to understand what the other person is experiencing. Listen and be sympathetic towards others.

3. **Set Healthy Boundaries**: Identify your limits and state them clearly. Healthy boundaries guard your emotional well-being and deepen relationships.
4. **Enjoy Small Moments**: Love blossoms in the minutiae of daily life. Start little traditions to appreciate time shared with loved ones.
5. **Welcome Change**: Be open to new experiences and the organic changes that occur in a relationship. Growth often takes place in unexpected ways.
6. **Don't Be Afraid to Ask for Help**: Nobody has to go through the trials and tribulations of love alone. Don't be afraid to ask for help when feeling overwhelmed.

Let us then reaffirm our faith in the limitless strength of love. And through the care given to our relationships and through honouring that bond that we have for ourselves and others, a ripple effect comes from there beyond personal experiences. Every problem can be solved when approached with love, understanding, and patience.

As you travel through love—be it with partners, friends, or family—keep the spirit of optimism close to your heart. Keep hold of your self-worth. Enjoy the beauty of vulnerability. And don't forget to celebrate every step of the way in the journey of love. That's how you help build a world where love can be as free and wild as it wants to be, turning life from barely tolerable into something wonderfully beautiful.

As Rabindranath Tagore eloquently articulated, "**Love does not merely sing; it inspires.**" Allow your love to serve as an inspiration, a guiding force that nurtures those in your midst.

Following the profound wisdom of Swami Vivekananda, who asserted, "Where there is love, there is life," may your journey encapsulate the essence of love that infuses every moment with vitality.

Here's to love—may it be your guiding light, your greatest adventure, and the legacy you leave behind.

References

1. Bedson, B. (2014). Different Branches of the Same Tree Tree Planting day. Fox Creek Times, (), A.6.
2. Siddiqui, S. (2024). The lessons philanthropy can find in love. Indianapolis Business Journal, 44(51), 15D.
3. Nelson Mandela Quote: “Forgiveness liberates the soul. It removes fear. That is why it is such a powerful weapon.”. https://quotefancy.com/quote/874257/Nelson-Mandela-Forgiveness-liberates-the-soul-It-removes-fear-That-is-why-it-is-such-a
4. Love is the one thing we’re capable of perceiving that transcends dimensions of time and space. Maybe we should trust that, even if we can’t understand it. - HoopoeQuotes. https://www.hoopoequotes.com/movie-quotes/item/34249-love-is-the-one-thing-we-re-capable-of-perceiving-that-transcends-dimensions-of-time-and-space-maybe-we-should-trust-that-even-if-we-can-t-understand-it
5. 3 Ways You Can Successfully Get Out Of A Running Rut. https://www.womensrunning.com/health/3-ways-get-out-running-rut/?scope=anon
6. Paynich, V. “. (2022). Changemakers Remind Us of the Bigger Picture. Parks & Recreation, 57(12), 10.
7. Nayak, A. (2021). Revolution of technology in the new normal. International Journal of Advance Research, Ideas and Innovations in Technology. https://www.ijariit.com/manuscripts/v7i3/V7I3-1522.pdf

8. Howwouldyoudescribeyourwalkwith God in one word? - The Rebelution. https://www.therebelution.com/blog/2015/08/how-would-you-describe-your-walk-with-god-in-one-word/
9. Aces Integrative Therapy Blog | Spokane WA. https://acesintegrativetherapy.com/blog
10. Steidl, L. (2005). Chronický únavový syndrom. Interní Medicína pro Praxi. https://www.solen.cz/pdfs/int/2001/09/02.pdf
11. Success through Clutter Coaching – ReclaimYou. https://www.reclaimyou.net.nz/blogs/reclaimyou-blog/success-through-clutter-coaching
12. "Bhagavad Gita Chapter 2: Sankhya Yoga - Unveiling the Eternal Wisdom". https://www.divinecarefoundation.com/post/bhagavad-gita-chapter-2-sankhya-yoga-unveiling-the-eternal-wisdom
13. Olpin, Michael; Hesson, Margie (2009). Stress Management for Life (2nd ed.). Cengage Learning. p. 205. ISBN 978-0-324-59943-5.
14. Shanta Rameshwar Rao (1 January 1986). In Worship of Shiva. Orient Longman. pp. 29–. ISBN 978-0-86131-684-7.
15. "5 Love Languages for Lasting Inner Peace and Relationship Happiness". Zennout. Retrieved May 6, 2024.
16. Heidi R.M. Pauwels (17 December 2007). Indian Literature and Popular Cinema: Recasting Classics. Routledge. p. 80. ISBN 978-1-134-06255-3.

www.ingramcontent.com/pod-product-compliance
Lightning Source LLC
LaVergne TN
LVHW041216150826
845673LV00001B/419

* 9 7 8 9 3 6 7 0 7 1 2 4 3 *